Every leader in the new Emergent Movement will want to read this fascinating book. They simply will not find a more engaging, knowledgeable, balanced, and kind treatment of their concerns, ideas, and practices. R. Scott Smith is unique in his ability to see the Emergent Church in its broadest context and does a remarkable job of offering up key philosophical and theological insights that will help every follower of Christ live the Gospel.

—CRAIG J. HAZEN,
Professor of Comparative Religion, Biola University

The latest clarion call in the never-ending cavalcade of "what's new" in the evangelical world is the confident assertion from some quarters that the church needs to embrace "postmodernism" if it is going to engage postmodernity and postmoderns effectively. For those mystified, miffed, intrigued, or attracted by these claims, R. Scott Smith has supplied a helpful introduction and antidote in *Truth and the New Kind of Christian*. Smith here provides a useful entry-level overview of the way some are attempting to appropriate postmodernism for the church, and adds his own thoughtful appreciations, applications, and warnings. Thinking Christians who have been irritated by facile "postmodern" critiques of foundationalism, modernity, and "the old way of doing church" will find much light and encouragement here. Pastors who are trying to break down the often indigestible subject matter of postmodernism into bite-size chunks in order to equip their people to engage it, and teachers who are aiming at giving their students a working knowledge of the way postmodernism is impacting the church will find a good deal of help from Smith, who is structured, clear, and practical throughout.

—J. LIGON DUNCAN III,
Senior Minister, First Presbyterian Church, Jackson, Mississippi,
Adjunct Professor, Reformed Theological Seminary

Scott Smith and I agree on a lot. We share a deep commitment to Jesus Christ, a love of the Bible, and a passion for the church. We also agree that we're currently living in a liminal time, and it's those "boundary times" when people look most closely at the beliefs that underlie their practices. So, we've all got some things to figure out right now, including what we can really know and the certainty with which we can state our claims in a pluralistic society. I appreciate Scott's voice in this conversation. He is a careful reader of my work, and he writes with a gracious and generous tone. Interlocutors like Scott will be a helpful challenge to all of us in the "emerging church." I consider him a friendly critic and a brother in Christ.

—TONY JONES, author of *Postmodern Youth Ministry* and
National Director, Emergent

Scott Smith is uniquely suited to enter the Emergent conversation with this helpful volume, and I'm thankful that God has raised him up for such a time as this. Not only is he an analytic philosopher with a razor-sharp mind who has specialized in analyzing postmodernistic views on the relationship between language and the world, but he is also a man who cares for the lost, loves the church, and has an ability to communicate complex truths to people in the pew. I predict that Professor Smith's careful, patient, insightful interaction with Emergent presuppositions and arguments will gain him a wide hearing in this ongoing debate, for I am convinced that all of us—whatever our present opinion on the Emerging church—have something to learn from this wise and thoughtful book.

—JUSTIN TAYLOR, Executive Editor, Desiring God;
blogger (www.theologica.blogspot.com)

There is no more important issue facing the church than whether the message of the gospel corresponds to reality and therefore demands the attention of every single person. Scott Smith's study challenges us to take seriously the truth claim of the gospel both in how we proclaim it in words and in how we manifest it in our personal and community lives. I am grateful for this clarion call to maintain and proclaim with confidence the historic Christian gospel, which alone has saving power.

—GARY INRIG
Senior Pastor, Trinity Church, Redlands, California

the emerging effects of

postmodernism in the church

TRUTH
AND THE NEW KIND OF
CHRISTIAN

R. SCOTT SMITH

CROSSWAY BOOKS

A PUBLISHING MINISTRY OF
GOOD NEWS PUBLISHERS
WHEATON, ILLINOIS

Truth and the New Kind of Christian: The Emerging Effects of Postmodernism in the Church

Copyright © 2005 by R. Scott Smith

Published by Crossway Books
    a publishing ministry of Good News Publishers
    1300 Crescent Street
    Wheaton, Illinois 60187

Cover design: Jon McGrath

First printing 2005

Printed in the United States of America

Unless otherwise noted, Scripture quotations are from the *New American Standard Bible*® Copyright © The Lockman Foundation 1960, 1962, 1963, 1968, 1971, 1972, 1973, 1975, 1977. Used by permission.

Scripture references marked NIV are from the *Holy Bible: New International Version.*® Copyright © 1973, 1978, 1984 by International Bible Society. Used by permission of Zondervan Publishing House. All rights reserved.

The "NIV" and "New International Version" trademarks are registered in the United States Patent and Trademark Office by International Bible Society. Use of either trademark requires the permission of International Bible Society.

Library of Congress Cataloging-in-Publication Data
Smith, R. Scott, 1957-
    Truth and the new kind of Christian : the emerging effects of post-
modernism in the church / R. Scott Smith.
        p. cm.
    Includes bibliographical references and index.
    ISBN 1-58134-740-5 (trade pbk.)
    1. Postmodernism—Religious aspects—Christianity. 2. Postmodernism—
History. 3. Evangelicalism. I. Title.
BR115.P74S67   2005
230'.046—dc22   2005009090

VP		15	14	13	12	11	10	09	08	07	06	05
15	14	13	12	11	10	9	8	7	6	5	4	3	2	1

To my fellow members at Trinity Church
in Redlands, California,
and my graduate students in apologetics
at Biola University,
all lovers of the truth

CONTENTS

FOREWORD

I have known Scott Smith for fifteen years, and that knowledge convinces me that God has raised him up uniquely for such a time as this. We live in desperate times, with cultural confusion abounding. Our universities have failed us where we need them most: to speak loudly and clearly about spiritual and moral knowledge apt for connecting people with reality and thereby producing men and women with well-developed character. Instead, by and large, our universities have continued to perpetuate the myth that only science gives us truth and knowledge, whereas religious and ethical beliefs are just personal preferences, private opinions, and personal (or social) values.

We also live in a time in which the church itself needs clear guidance, and one crucial area in which it needs such help is in regards to what to think about postmodernism. For many Christians, they have heard of postmodernism, and they may know something of its influence on their children. But they often know little about its specific ideas, or how it is being promoted by certain Christian thinkers. Other Christians, however, have become quite enamored with, and influenced by, postmodern thought and style, and these believers see much promise not only for reaching a postmodern culture with the gospel but also for rethinking the faith itself along postmodern lines.

Enter Scott Smith. With graduate training in metaphysics, epistemology, philosophy of mind and language, and ethics, he brings a specialization in postmodern thought to the task of providing our community with the leadership necessary to guide us in responding to the postmodern turn in a Christ- and truth-honoring way. Make no mistake about it. This book is simply a must read for anyone with a heart for God, the teaching of the Bible, and the needs of a lost culture. Smith deftly takes us on a tour of postmodernism in general, and Christian postmodernism in particular. He then spells out in detail the impact of postmodernism on youth ministry, the university, and the church. Not content to stop with analysis, he provides a clear assessment of crucial aspects of postmodernism *in* the church as well as its specific influence on the Emerging Church, as seen in the writings of Brian McLaren and Tony Jones. I wholeheartedly would encourage readers of all kinds (whether or not they have been strongly influenced by postmodern ideas) to dialogue with Scott Smith in response to his ideas.

I could not recommend this book more highly. Smith is to be thanked for writing this book, and God is to be thanked for raising him up for such a time as this.

—J. P. Moreland
Distinguished Professor of Philosophy
Talbot School of Theology
Biola University

PREFACE

This book is an outworking of my longstanding interest in understanding and addressing postmodernism. When I was explaining my dissertation to a fellow evangelical graduate student at the University of Southern California, he suggested that I should develop a version of the same project for a church audience. I also have been explaining postmodernism to classes at my church and at Biola University and have found myself becoming more and more interested in helping believers understand postmodernism and how it is at work in our churches.

Then, over the course of a few years, through presenting papers at the Evangelical Theological Society's national conferences, I saw that certain evangelicals were trying to influence their peers (and their students and fellow church members) to reconceive the faith along postmodern lines. While I saw them point out various strengths of postmodernism, their criticisms of "modernism" were far less than convincing. Indeed, I did not see them address (much less even recognize) what I think are the core issues involved with adopting a postmodern understanding of our faith.

It is one thing to write and lecture to graduate students about postmodernism; it is another to talk about it to church audiences. So, over time, I became convinced that I needed to do just that. I talked with various people at my church to get their feedback on my ideas, and I spoke to lay audiences at our apologetics lectures at Biola University. This book has grown out of those experiences and my study.

My hope and prayer in writing this book is that God will use it greatly to enable Christians to carefully understand both the strengths and the weaknesses of postmodernism—in particular Christian postmodernism and how that is being expressed in the Emerging Church—and in that understanding to see which aspects of it we should embrace and which ones we must resist and even reject.

My deep thanks go to several people. First, Rob Bleakney, a fellow graduate student at the University of Southern California, first suggested to me that there was an additional market for the ideas I originally developed in my dissertation and subsequent book, *Virtue Ethics and Moral Knowledge: Philosophy of Language After MacIntyre and Hauerwas* (Ashgate, 2003). Second, I am indebted to J. P. Moreland and Dallas Willard for the model they gave me in their lives, for their love for Christ, and for their deep philosophical insights. Third, I am thankful for the encouragement and insights of my director at Biola, Craig Hazen, who has given me many opportunities to address this topic with our students. Fourth, I deeply appreciate my fellow members and pastors at Trinity Evangelical Free Church in Redlands, California. We are part of a church in which people really want to understand the faith and the reasons why we should believe it. I have been greatly encouraged by the rich teaching of our senior pastor, Gary Inrig, and our former senior associate pastor, Rick Langer.

Fifth, several of our graduate students at Biola have been most helpful in their encouragement, feedback on drafts of chapters, and enthusiasm for this topic. Thanks especially to Stan Jantz, Brad Fox, and Josh Shoemaker. Sixth, I have been helped in my understanding of postmodernism from conversations with and/or books by Tony Jones, Steve Sherman, Brad Kallenberg, and others. Thanks! Seventh, Justin Taylor of Desiring God has given me much helpful feedback and encouragement, for which I am most grateful. Eighth, Jim Weaver provided helpful chapter title suggestions. Ninth, I am deeply grateful for Bill Deckard's very helpful editorial suggestions, which have helped me express several ideas much more clearly than otherwise would have been the case. Thanks also to Noah Dennis, Bill's colleague at Crossway, for his editorial help.

Most of all, I want to express my deep, abiding love for my wife, Debbie, and our daughter, Anna. You are the two most precious people in my life!

—R. Scott Smith
Masters of Arts Program in Christian Apologetics
Biola University

INTRODUCTION

CHRISTIAN RELATIVISTS

It is obvious in Western society that many people think moral and religious truths are relative. Not only is this idea clearly taught in secular universities, our media also trumpet it. But it has not been the position of historic, orthodox Christianity. In that light, it is surprising how many Christians now think that way as well. For example, a Barna poll showed that, even after the terrorist attacks on September 11, only 32 percent of born-again Christian adults, and a mere 9 percent of born-again Christian teens, think that ethics are *not* relative.[1] Christians are increasingly accepting of ethical relativism, and in a climate that promotes pluralism, we are losing our understanding of Christian ethical and religious truths as being *objectively* true.

What do I mean by something being objectively true? Objective truths are true for all people, whether or not anyone accepts them as true or talks about them as such. Their status as being true (that is, corresponding with how things are in reality) is independent of our knowing them to be true. For example, 2+2=4 is objectively true in that its truth value is independent of anyone's believing it or not. Similarly, murder is wrong even if someone happens to say otherwise.

Not surprisingly, the large decline in the percentage of Christians who hold to the objective character of morals mirrors what has been going on in our culture, and especially on our secular campuses, for some time now. When I first stepped onto the campus at the University of Southern California in Los Angeles as a graduate student, I sensed very clearly that the dominant view there was that all ethical and religious views are relative. As I both studied and taught there from 1995 to 2000, this impression was confirmed by repeated experiences with

---

[1] See "Americans Are Most Likely to Base Truth on Feelings," online, www.barna.org, February 12, 2002, accessed September 24, 2002.

professors, reading assignments, fellow graduate students, and my own first-year students.

The secular universities (and, to varying extents, some Christian ones too) have divided basically into two vastly different schools of thought. By and large, the humanities have accepted the idea that truth is up to us, while the hard sciences (and maybe still business, insofar as it tries to operate as a science) attempt to give us the objective truth about the world. According to this view, science gives us facts, but religion and morals, in particular, give us mere opinions, personal tastes, and values. This is evidence of what has been called the "fact-value dichotomy," a view that has been with us at least since the time of Immanuel Kant (1724–1804). In the face of the claims of modern science, especially those of atheistic evolution, society and academia have marginalized Christian truth claims as being just opinions. They are seen as nonscientific and therefore not on the same par as scientific claims.

I knew that my first-year students at USC would tend to assume that ethics are relative. In light of this mind-set, I deliberately challenged that belief. I would give them an assignment in which they had to argue to what extent ethical relativism is right. They would read an article written by a secular philosopher that exposes the many severe problems with relativism, which made it an excellent choice to use with a secular audience.[2] Then I would have them consult with me about their rough drafts. In reading their drafts, I often would discover which of the students were Christians, and even which of those had attended Christian high schools. Yet in four years of giving that assignment, I found only three such students who were prepared to challenge relativism. Only two could give philosophical reasons against relativism, of which there are many, and the other was able only to quote Scripture against it.

But among the other Christian students, I often found an attitude that while Christianity is true, who are we to impose our beliefs on

---

[2] I used the chapter titled "Ethical Relativism: Who's to Say What's Right or Wrong?" in Louis Pojman's *Ethics: Discovering Right and Wrong*, 4th ed. (Belmont, Mass.: Wadsworth, 2001). While I endorse Pojman's chapter on relativism, I am not nearly so enthusiastic about his chapter in defense of objective moral truths. He tries to tie a defense of universal moral truths with naturalistic evolution, a very dubious project at best.

someone else? They too had bought into the cultural ethos of tolerance based on relativism. Their Christian high schools and churches had done little to challenge this thinking or prepare them to deal with relativism. But what was very interesting to me was that after we discussed the secular philosopher's article at length, nearly all students, including the secular ones, rejected relativism as the whole truth of the matter! They realized that at least some morals have to be objectively true.

BUT CAN WE KNOW OBJECTIVE TRUTH?

As Western Christians are buying into relativism more and more, this attitude threatens to completely eviscerate our historic stance on having objective truth based on God's unchanging character and His revelation in the Bible. Now there is another view in our universities, both secular and even many Christian ones, and in our churches as well. It calls into question our ability to know objective truth. This view is *postmodernism*.

As I spent more time at USC, I focused my studies on postmodernism and wrote my dissertation on a key aspect of it. I found in the secular university classrooms and academic books that the humanities (including subjects such as religion, English, education, linguistics, art, history, sociology, and many more) have, by and large, accepted postmodernism's key philosophical ideas. Postmodernism may seem similar to, yet it is different from, ethical relativism. Ethical relativists think that there are no objective moral truths, things that are in fact true for all people across all cultures. Some postmodernists might hold that view, but most hold to something similar yet different: *even if* objective truths exist, say the postmodernists, we cannot *know* them as such.

Interestingly, some Christians are advocating that we should understand the faith in a postmodern way. I have found that there are at least two emphases they make. For one, several emphasize that we need to "contextualize" the faith in ways that will enable us to reach postmodern people, especially people of generations "X" and "Y." These people have been very influenced by postmodern thought and attitudes, these Christians maintain, so if we are to reach them with the gospel, we must find ways to contextualize Christianity that postmodern people will appreciate and understand.

A second emphasis is more theoretical, and it is that we should not only contextualize the faith, we also should postmodernize the faith itself. Here we see the work of the more philosophical ideas driving postmodern thought, and this is where I want to assess carefully the postmoderns' recommendations. We will see much of the theoretical work being done by people like Nancey Murphy, the late Stanley Grenz, John Franke, Brad Kallenberg, and even Stanley Hauerwas. We also will find that Brian McLaren, perhaps the most influential leader of the Emerging Church, and Tony Jones, recently appointed national coordinator of Emergent U.S., draw upon and may argue for certain theoretical ideas, but more so, they are concerned about how believers need to embody and embrace postmodern ideas and values in order to be truly faithful to the Lord in these times. This is what McLaren means by the title of his widely influential book, *A New Kind of Christian*. In his view, living out Christianity in a "modern" way just will not cut it in postmodern times, and it also will leave aside many postmodern people who will not hear the gospel if it is preached and lived out in modern ways.

For many Christians, though, I believe there is a general lack of understanding about postmodernism and in particular Christian postmodernism. When I have taught on this topic at church or school events, I have found that many believers think they should be concerned about postmodernism but they have little or no idea about its main ideas. This is especially so among Christian parents, but even their teenage children have little conception of what postmodernism is. And I have found many Christian adults are utterly surprised to hear that some Christians are advocating a postmodern way of interpreting our faith.

Recently I spoke to a graduate-level class for youth workers at my school, Biola University. They had read a text on postmodernism and youth ministry, which happens to have been written by Tony Jones, whose views we will examine. While they realized that they need to address the postmodern mind-set of many youth, they also lacked the tools to assess Jones's views. Indeed, many youth ministers themselves have been influenced to approach ministry and their faith in a postmodern way.

TWO KINDS OF POSTMODERNISM

It will be helpful to first get a big-picture view of postmodernism, in order to understand its main ideas. There are two levels of postmodernism at work in society. First, there is the *"street"* or *popular* level, in which postmodernism manifests itself in attitudes such as *suspicion of authorities' claims* to be telling the truth or to be acting for the good of people. Instead, postmodern ways of thinking have led us to realize that leaders often are acting to preserve their own power. After all, we know that Richard Nixon covered up the White House's involvement in Watergate, just to preserve his presidency. Bill Clinton stretched our commonsense understanding when he claimed that he smoked marijuana but did not inhale, and that he did not have sexual relations with Monica Lewinsky. Clinton carefully crafted his meanings of these words to protect himself from criticism or even impeachment.

This same distrust of authorities often manifests itself in a deep *suspicion of hierarchies*. Often I saw this attitude in my fellow graduate students who had had a Catholic upbringing. They were angry at the Catholic emphasis on a church hierarchy that could give normative ethical and theological pronouncements for all Catholics. This same distrust of hierarchies is often evidenced in feminist writings as well. But distrust is not limited to just religious hierarchies; for example, many who opposed the Vietnam War were motivated by deep suspicions of the motives of the U.S. government in waging the war. Today, people are routinely suspicious of the motives of corporate executives who lay off large numbers of employees only to vote themselves enormous bonuses.

Postmodern attitudes have also been shaped by a *distrust of modern science*. Confidence in the goodness of science was shattered when we discovered how the Nazis used medical science to perform gross experiments on Jewish subjects. Scientists also developed the most destructive weapon we know to date, the nuclear bomb. People now are far less trusting of scientists' claims to be acting solely for the good of humanity. People are tempted to abuse their power, and we are rightly suspicious of claims made by the powerful that they are acting solely for the good of others. We often question their vested interests, as well we should.

Another key trait of postmodernism "on the street" is very noticeable among our youth. More than anything, I think, they are looking for "authentic" people. They do not want just promises; they are looking for people whose lives and deeds match up with their words.

How and where do we find authentic lives? The postmodern answer is *we find it in community.* Instead of supporting a rugged individualism, which still dominates much of American society, postmoderns look for authentic people in communities. This is the kind of attitude shift that Robert Bellah and his coauthors suggested in their widely read sociological book *Habits of the Heart,* where they observed that people are looking for places of belonging that may be the primary basis for the formation of their sense of identity.[3]

These attitudes help show why postmodernism is attractive to some Christians. For one, the attitude of suspicion toward authorities' truth claims resonates with our understanding that all people are sinners and are capable of great deception, self-interest, and quests for power. For another, some Christians find a natural parallel between the postmodern emphasis on living in community and the "one another" biblical teachings. That is, they see the church as the Christian community in which we are to live out the life of Christ as a witness to outsiders.

When you draw together these values and attitudes, a common thread emerges. On a popular, everyday level, most people think that science gives us the facts about the physical world. Scientists still enjoy that prestige. When the person in the scientist's white lab coat advertises a product, that endorsement gives the product credibility. But there is a vast split in people's minds between the facts that science can give and the values or preferences that religion and ethics provide. And, most importantly for our purposes in this study, people tend to think that ethical and religious truth claims are simply *up to us.* According to the popular, street-level version of postmodernism, there is no factual, objective religious or ethical truth that we all can know and that is true for everyone. It used to be that Christians could approach someone and read through a booklet like *The Four Spiritual Laws,* and there would be a common basis for understanding those biblical truths. While that still will happen with some people, it now is becoming more common that

---

[3] Robert Bellah, Richard Madsen, William M. Sullivan, Ann Swidler, and Steven M. Tipton, *Habits of the Heart* (New York: Harper & Row, 1986).

someone would merely reply, "That is a nice story. Now let me tell you my story!"

That is street postmodernism, but there is also *academic postmodernism*. Academic postmoderns are highly suspicious of human reason's abilities. In fact, while many "modernists" (a term relating to the modern era, or the Enlightenment, roughly 1550–1945) thought that we could know universal, objective truths by our reason, postmodernists have given up on knowing such truths. This is an *epistemological* claim, which simply is a claim about what we can know and how we can know. Instead of knowing the world as it really is, academic postmoderns claim that we cannot know any such thing. We are left with having to "make," or shape, our own worlds ourselves, including religious and ethical "truths." Notice that this is a *metaphysical* claim, meaning that it is a claim about the nature of what exists.

How do we make our own worlds? We do it in community, or culture, say the postmoderns, and we use the *language* of our community to make our world. This touches on a key element of both academic and street postmodernism: the focus has shifted away from the rugged individual, still very popular in American society, to the community. This emphasis on community is enticing to some Christian academic postmodernists, for they want to say that the true community is the church, and the language of the church is the Gospels, which are written in a narrative, story-like format. With an emphasis on language and on how we talk in community, postmoderns stress narratives, or stories. One result of this is that the terminology within our churches is changing from someone telling his or her testimony, to telling his or her *story*.

One implication of academic postmodernism is that if we cannot know reality (how things really are), then we cannot know what an author (of a book in the Bible, the Constitution, etc.) really meant. Thus, in many Bible studies, a frequently asked question is, "What does the passage mean *to you?*" as though we cannot know what Paul, Luke, or Peter meant when they wrote a book. Now, somewhat subtly, even if this question is asked unintentionally, the implication seems to be that the meaning of the passage is up to us, a meaning that we must *make for ourselves*.

Clearly, postmodernism undermines any claims to know objective truth, and when applied to Christian truth claims, this approach would seem to offer a serious challenge to the Christian faith. But is that the case? To what extent should we (or should we not) as Christians embrace the ideas of the Emerging Church and other Christian post-modernists? Christian postmodernism is more problematic than the postmodernism offered by non-Christians, since writers such as Stanley Hauerwas (a theological ethicist), Stanley Grenz and John Franke (evangelical theologians), and Brad Kallenberg (an evangelical philosophical theologian) all will say that the gospel is the truth. In this they are right, but what they mean by this is not that it is the objective, universal truth for all people, which can be known as such. They believe we cannot know such things. Instead, they say, the claims that the gospel is the true story or that Jesus is the only way to God are true because these are the ways we as Christians should *talk* according to our "grammar," the Bible. By looking at Christian postmodernism, we can clarify specific implications of this view for Christians and Christianity, and we also can gain insights into postmodernism more broadly conceived.

So I will address several aspects of Christian postmodernism and assess to what extent Christians should, or should not, embrace it. I believe we will find both strengths and weaknesses in Christian post-modernism, and in the proposals offered by McLaren and Jones of the Emerging Church in particular. To do that, I will try to give a brief background to help us understand better how we have shifted from a once-dominant understanding that ethics and religious claims are objectively true, to a view that they are relative, and now to a postmodern view that they are just what communities (or cultures) have created. These are the emphases of chapter 1, where I will also compare the modern period with our postmodern one.

In chapter 2, I will explain how postmodernists like Hauerwas, Grenz, Franke, and Kallenberg think we should see Christianity in a postmodern way. In chapter 3, we will look at how and why two leaders of the very influential Emerging Church, Brian McLaren and Tony Jones, advocate a postmodern approach to the faith, especially in pastoral ministry. Chapter 4 will explain how postmodernism is surfacing within academic departments in secular and Christian universities, to help us see the extent of its influences as well as begin to examine them.

Then, in chapter 5, we will begin a critique of Christian postmodernism, and postmodernism more generally conceived. I will criticize postmodernism's core philosophical ideas. In chapter 6, I will assess the extent to which we should accept McLaren and Jones's proposals as leaders of the Emerging Church. In chapter 7, I will continue to address the implications of postmodernism for Christian ethics and several essential Christian doctrines. Having shown the need for Christians to reject key aspects (but not all) of postmodernism—particularly as Christians conceive it—in chapter 8 I will look at the issue of relativism. Is postmodernism just relativism in new clothing? If it is, is that a serious problem? I also will try to address why Christians are attracted to, but should not embrace, relativism, despite the appeals and pressures in our culture to be tolerant and open-minded.

Overall, I will try to show that we have no good reason to give up the objectivity of Christian truths by accepting certain postmodern ideas, especially in a day when the objective character of Christian beliefs is under assault. So, in chapter 9, I will develop my own positive case why I think we can (and often do) know objective truth in morality, religion, history, and other areas. Finally, I have provided a bibliography of materials (books, tapes, websites, etc.) available for further study on postmodernism. I have categorized these according to their level of difficulty as well as by topic.

If Paul was right (and I believe he was) that in Jesus Christ are hidden all the treasures of wisdom and knowledge (Col. 2:3), we need not, even dare not, abandon the objective truth of the Scriptures. Instead, we can stand firm, being fully assured that our faith and its many claims are objectively true, and that we can know it to be so. Further, and contrary to McLaren, we need not have "bombproof" certainty to know that Christianity's claims are true.[4]

It is true, of course, that truth can be used as a club. May that not be the case. We need to heed the postmodern reminder that truth must be embodied, or lived out. And we must match our embodiment of truth with the embodiment of grace, just as it was in the life of Christ (John 1:14). We need to live out both grace and truth, which I think will make for a very powerful witness in these postmodern times.

---

[4] See Brian McLaren, *More Ready Than You Realize* (Grand Rapids, Mich.: Zondervan, 2002), 131.

"If you abide in My word,
then you are truly disciples of Mine;
and you shall know the truth, and the truth
shall make you free."

JESUS, JOHN 8:31-32

"As Christians we claim that by conforming
our lives in a faithful manner to the stories of God
we acquire the moral and intellectual skills,
as a community and as individuals,
to face the world as it is, not as we wish it to be.
Of course this remains a 'claim,' for there is no way
within history to prove that such a story must be true."

STANLEY HAUERWAS
A COMMUNITY OF CHARACTER, 96

ONE

WHAT IS POSTMODERNISM?

Like any philosophical and cultural view, postmodernism did not arise in a vacuum. It has a history. To help get a better handle on what its views are and how it affects us today, both academically and "on the street," we need to take a brief look at some historical factors that helped give rise to postmodernism. Along the way, we will define some terms and explain key ideas. Then we will be in a position to explain what postmodernism is, in light of the views it repudiates.

FROM THE ANCIENTS TO THE REFORMATION

For the better part of two millennia, most Western philosophers and theologians held to the objective character of ethics and religion. They did not think that these truths were relative to individuals or cultures, but instead that they were universally true and applicable to all people. That is, they are objectively true, whether or not anyone accepts them as true.

Plato and Aristotle

This is the kind of view we see in Plato (427–347 B.C.), who held that in the realm of the ideal, the *forms* are absolute, universal truths, and we are to conform our lives to those ideals. Aristotle (384–322 B.C.) took Plato's ideas and adapted them, but he did not abandon Plato's concept of the forms. While Plato thought we know these ideal truths by *deductive* reasoning, Aristotle believed we know them by *inductive* reasoning.[1]

---

[1] An example of deductive reasoning is: All bachelors are unmarried males. Jones is an unmarried male. So Jones is a bachelor. The conclusion (that Jones is a bachelor) must follow from the premises. With inductive reasoning, you draw an inference from various premises. For example, this raven is black. Another raven is black, and so is a third raven, and also a fourth. Therefore, we infer that all ravens are black.

While he emphasized looking at particular people and things to know what these truths are, they still are, on his view, universally true.

Both Plato and Aristotle were virtue ethicists. This means that they stressed the character qualities of the person, and the good person lives out the "cardinal" virtues of prudence, temperance, courage, and justice. Importantly, they thought these were universally valid character qualities that all people should develop, so they did not see these as mere social conventions. In this sense, both Plato and Aristotle were *realists;* they thought that there are traits that really exist that are normative for all people, and that we can know them as such.

In addition, they thought that human beings have a goal toward which they should aim, which in Greek is called the *telos.* This is not the idea of a mere career objective, or some ambitions in life, but rather it is the idea that there is a normative, ethical standard that all of us should strive to emulate in terms of our character.

New Testament Ethics

Interestingly, the New Testament emphasizes similar concepts. In addition to its emphasis on keeping the principles and commands of Jesus, the New Testament writers also emphasize the importance of *becoming like Christ*. Here, the virtues are revealed by God as the character qualities of Jesus, such as those listed in Galatians 5:22-23, where we are encouraged to grow in love, joy, peace, patience, and more. Importantly, these are qualities that are normative for all people.

We may see these concepts in several places. For instance, in Philippians 2:5ff., Paul tells us that we are to have the same attitude that Christ had when He humbled Himself and did not regard equality with God a thing to be grasped. Paul's letters are filled with such an emphasis, for his typical pattern in his letters is to first give doctrine and then give practical exhortations and teaching as to how we are to live out those truths. After instructing the Ephesians for the first three chapters about the blessings of redemption and what God has done for them, he then tells them that they are to imitate God, and walk in love, just as Christ loved them (5:1-2). Then comes a series of commands about qualities that should *not* be part of their lives, in contrast to those that should be (e.g., no immorality, no filthiness, but rather thankfulness). And in chapter 4,

Paul tells the Ephesians that there is a goal for the body of Christ, along with each member in it: that we attain "the knowledge of the Son of God, to a mature man, to the measure of the stature which belongs to the fulness of Christ" (4:13). He repeats the same concept in Colossians 1:28: "And we proclaim Him, admonishing every man and teaching every man with all wisdom, that we may present every man complete in Christ." Being *complete* indicates the idea that we become mature (or, perfect), having reached our goal, which is to become like Jesus.

Paul wants all believers to reach their maturity, which is Christlikeness, and it is not just an individual project. Instead, it requires our living out our relationship with Jesus with other believers, together with whom we may glorify Him. God has given believers certain spiritual gifts for the building up of the whole body (Eph. 4:13). First John also picks up this focus on the body of Christ with John's many exhortations to love one another. Paul stresses these "one anothers" when he commands the Christians at Colossae to "put on a heart of compassion, kindness, humility, gentleness and patience; bearing with one another, and forgiving each other" (3:12-13). In the New Testament, the moral life is not separated from the "body life" of the church.

So living in community (i.e., the church) becomes a vital theme in New Testament ethics, as does becoming like Jesus. Commands are still front and center, too. For instance, in the Sermon on the Mount, Jesus did not nullify the Law; rather, He came to fulfill it (Matt. 5:17). Commands are interpreted so that actions and intentions matter, and these involve compassion for people and not just a rigid adherence to principles. The way we understand what it means to be like Christ often is given by way of command, as we just saw in Colossians 3:12-13.

Thomas Aquinas and the Middle Ages, and the Reformation

After Christianity became the dominant worldview of the West, theologians and philosophers tended to affirm a belief in universal, objective truth. They grounded this belief not only in the biblical revelation but also in philosophical thought. During the Middle Ages, Muslims rediscovered the writings of Aristotle, and after a lengthy absence, other theologians started to look at ways Aristotelian philosophy, with its confidence in human reason, could be employed to better understand the world. Thomas Aquinas (1225–1274) synthesized Augustinian theology with Aristotelian philosophy in order to ground his more speculative theological claims and his ethics. Importantly, these were objective in nature for him, and they were known not just by human reason but also by special revelation. Aquinas had an ethic that was applicable for all people. That is, though undergirded by divine revelation, he had a way to hold nonbelievers accountable, ethically speaking, since by reason there are things we all know are wrong, such as murder, rape, and genocide.

But Aquinas also held to a theological view that humans were not so radically fallen that our reasoning abilities could not be trusted. He held that we are to obey God, and furthermore, we are capable by nature to obey Him. In the Fall, said Aquinas, we lost the miracle of grace, but we did not become so radically corrupted as the Reformers would later teach. According to his view, our primary problem is not sin but the loss of grace. Accordingly, our greatest need is for grace, which God gives us through the sacraments. It was this kind of view of our fallen condition that led to Aquinas's high confidence in our ability to use our reason to know truth. And it would be a confidence in reason that would be used by later thinkers to discount any need for special revelation.

However, in the Reformation we first see a shift from too much confidence being placed in human reasoning to a stronger emphasis on human sinfulness and the utter need for divine revelation. Hence, the Reformers stressed *"sola scriptura"* without the extra reliance on tradition and reason typical of Catholic thinkers. John Calvin and Martin Luther strongly held to the objective nature of Christianity, as well as its rational character, being witnessed both by general revelation (in the creation) and by special revelation (Scripture).

. . . and into the Enlightenment

But when we come into the Age of the Enlightenment, or the "modern" era (roughly 1550 to perhaps 1945),[2] there were two key

---

[2] I suggest 1945 as a date for the end of the modern era and the beginning of the postmodern one since this marks two major events that undermined people's confidence in the goodness of science. The "promise" of the Enlightenment's high view of science was that science not only gives us the truth about the world but that it will enable us to make inevitable progress for the betterment of humankind. But then came the death camps of the Nazis and their use of scientific experiments upon people, as well as

breaks that took place. First, *rationalism* emphasized the adequacy of human reason to know objective, rational truths. René Descartes (1596–1650) is one thinker who strongly exuded such confidence. No longer was there a perceived need for special revelation from the Bible to give us universal truths. This move was precipitated in part by Thomas Hobbes (1588–1679), who played off Aquinas's confidence in unaided human reason's ability to know truth. Hobbes drew the natural conclusion that if human reason is so adequate, why do we need the Bible to tell us how we should live, or to give us other kinds of truth? With this growing confidence in human reason's ability to know universal truths, special revelation seemed unnecessary. Philosophically, confidence in science to give us truths without reference to Christian theology began to gain credence.

A second major break from the past that took place in the modern period was the rise of *empiricism*. This is the view that we can know only what we can touch, taste, smell, see, or hear. Of course we all recognize the validity of empirical knowledge, which simply is knowledge we have by using our senses. Empiricism, however, limits *all* knowledge to that which comes by way of the five senses. So, several things that we used to think we could know could no longer be known! For instance, God cannot be seen, for He is spirit. Since the empiricists insist that all knowledge comes by way of the five senses, God, for them, is not the kind of thing about which we can have rational beliefs. Moral and religious truths, such as virtuous character qualities, or our souls and their fallen condition, also were seen as no longer things we could know to be true, because they too were not the kinds of things we could see, touch, and so forth.

David Hume (1711–1776)

While Hobbes applied empiricism to his political and ethical ideas, the other British empiricists, John Locke, Bishop George Berkeley, and

---

the atom bomb. Science has been used, even under the guise of experiments for the supposed good of people, as an instrument of death, oppression, and gross evil. The confidence in the goodness and inevitable progress of science started to give way to the more postmodern attitude of suspicion.

David Hume, developed empiricist thought. While Locke and Berkeley were Christians and tried to keep room for God's existence and some sort of contact with reality, Hume went much further in his conclusions by pushing empiricism in a much more consistent manner. For Hume, we are "trapped" behind our sense experiences, such as discrete appearances of colors, smells, sounds, and so forth. According to Hume, we cannot know anything in a so-called "real" world. In fact, all that we think exists in our everyday world (like cars, chairs, tables, computers, chicken dinners, and even other people) are just *projections* of the mind. Inspired by his empiricism, Hume developed his skeptical arguments against God's existence, such as his famous argument against miracles. And he presented a radical change in how to understand morals. For him, they are just our passions, and reason is their slave, to serve them.

Immanuel Kant (1724–1804)

Obviously, if Hume's empiricism were left unchallenged, then what we can know, including God's existence and the objectivity of moral truths, would be severely limited. So empiricism presented a serious challenge to reason, especially the kind defended by earlier Enlightenment thinkers. Immanuel Kant attempted to answer Hume's empiricism in order to defend rationalism, including the objective character of ethics. But his approach was doomed to failure early on, for he accepted Hume's basic idea that all knowledge comes by way of the five senses. So reason was handicapped right from the start in Kant's view.

Kant's attempted answer becomes an important precursor to current postmodern ideas. For him, we cannot know things in themselves, which he called the *noumenal* world, but only things as they appear to us, which is the *phenomenal* world. To put it differently, we cannot know objective reality (what he would call the *noumena*); we only know how it appears to us (the *phenomena*). There is always something that stands between us and the real world, and it is our sense experiences of the world. How then does Kant think we can gain objectivity?

According to Kant, we (as individuals) are trapped
behind our experiences, and we cannot know things as they
really are (in themselves).

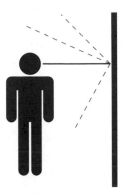

Reality
(the noumenal world)

He posits a transcendental mind that does the same work in each of us,
by constructing the world of our experience, including chairs, desks,
buildings, people, and so on.

Kant's views helped to develop another key idea that is very influential today: science gives us knowledge and facts, but other disciplines,
such as religion, can only give us values, or personal opinions and tastes.
For empiricism, all knowledge comes from the five senses, and the so-called scientific method tended to use an empirical means to discover
truths about the world. So, under Kant's view, science took off, getting
the philosophical prestige that it still enjoys today. However, according
to Kant's view, we cannot sense God with the five senses, so God cannot be known to exist. The same goes for having free wills, as well as
souls. But personally, Kant was not prepared to give these up, so he
posited that we must act *as if* these things were true. But the dividing
line had been drawn: science gives us truth, while religion gives us an
inferior sort of knowledge, at best. Even though Kant tried to preserve
the objectivity of morals, his empiricist ideas would not spare morality
from the same fate as religion in the minds of later thinkers.

. . . and into the "Linguistic Turn"

Several thinkers who followed Kant began to get tired of empiricism's
idea that we are stuck behind our sense experiences. Friedrich Nietzsche

(1844–1900) was the first one to introduce the idea that *language* somehow is involved in the process of how we know the world. Later on, the atheist Bertrand Russell (1872–1970) developed his idea of a formal language that we use to help make the world. But in the early twentieth century, people like Ludwig Wittgenstein (1889–1951) and Martin Heidegger (1889–1976) made the break explicit. No longer was it thought that we are "stuck" behind our experiences and cannot get "outside" to the real world. Instead, they developed the idea that we are on the "inside" of *language* and cannot know reality. I will try to explain this core idea in the next chapter. For now, let us notice that this shift in emphasis in philosophy from experience to language is what is called the linguistic turn, and it marks a turn toward postmodern thought.

There are several core philosophical ideas driving postmodern thought:

1. There is a real world that exists, but all we can know about it is what we know by our talking about it.
2. This is because we are on the "inside" of language and cannot get out to know the real world as it truly (i.e., objectively) is.
3. There are no universal truths that we may know—true for all people in all places at all times. If we could know such things, this would mean that we could know some things that are true regardless of language use. But that is not possible.
4. Thus, there is no essence, or nature, to language. There are only many languages.
5. Meaning is not a matter of what a person meant by a statement, that is, his or her intentions in making the statement. If it were, we each could have that same intention in our minds. But that would mean that there is a universal truth we could know apart from how we use language. Instead, meaning is just a matter of how words are used within a social setting, or community, according to the grammatical rules for its language.
6. Since we cannot know the real world as it truly is, and our only contact with it is by how we talk, each community "makes" its own social world by the use of its language.

The postmodern view is similar to Kant's kind of thought. No longer is it the case that we *individually* cannot know things in themselves, or as they really are, but only as they appear to each of us. Instead, we (*together,* in community, and not privately) cannot know reality as it truly is, *but only as we talk about it in our respective communities.*

Furthermore, each community has its own language, and the members within a community construct their world by the proper use of their language. So, there are as many worlds as there are communities and languages. There is at least one Christian world,[3] as well as a Muslim world, a Buddhist one, a Hindu one, a secularist one, a Mormon one, and many, many others.

Academic postmodernism:
Language stands between us and the world.

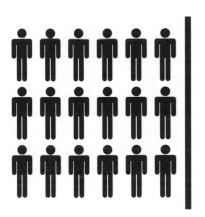

Objective
reality

COMPARING THE MODERN AND POSTMODERN ERAS

The postmodern emphasis is on the use of language to "make," or "construct," our own worlds. But as its name indicates, postmodernism is a response to modernism, or the Enlightenment. Let us summarize some of the key differences between postmodernism and its predecessor. First, the modern era emphasized the confidence that human reason, apart from divine revelation, could know universal truths in all subject matters. But postmodernism stresses the fallibility of human reason, as well as its biases and how it all too often is used to oppress people. By stress-

---

[3] Later, however, I will argue that Christians are not so homogeneous as to be able to hold (as claimed in the view we are considering) that there is just one Christian world, or Christian community.

ing the fallible nature of human reasoning, postmodernism has a key point of contact with the Christian doctrine of sin, as well as our understanding of our limitations as finite, created beings.

People in the modern era also tended to believe in the inevitability of progress, because of the amazing discoveries of science and also because of inferences from the theory of evolution. Humankind could become better and better, or so it was thought. But the twentieth century helped shatter that illusion with two world wars, the concentration and extermination camps, genocides, and the nuclear bomb. We saw how the Soviet myth of the greatness of its social system was exploded by the brutal reality of the Stalinist gulags, as well as the utter decay of the economies of the Iron Curtain countries.

The confident attitudes of the modern era also meant that we tended to trust our political and religious leaders. But now we are living many years after Watergate, CIA cover-ups, the Jim Bakker scandal, and the sex scandals that have rocked the Roman Catholic Church. Such betrayals of the public trust have only confirmed postmodern attitudes of suspicion.

A key part of life today is the emphasis on pluralism. In the modern view of the world, we thought we could find objective, universal truths that applied to all people. There were thought to be normative ways for all cultures to live. Now, however, in a postmodern era, that idea would seem "quaint" at best and oppressive and imperialistic at worst. Indeed, starting at least with Vietnam, Americans began to question the motives for our involvement economically and militarily in other countries. Instead, it was concluded, we need to be tolerant of different cultures, ways of living, and morals, for there is no universal standard we can know that is true for all people. Thus, we are not to oppress others by imposing our values on them.

With the postmodern emphasis on communities (or cultures) and their languages, the need for authentic lives in those communities, as well as the attitude of suspicion, it is natural that we should see a variety of different postmodern views surface. And that is exactly the case; there are secular postmodern writers (e.g., Richard Rorty), who celebrate the so-called death of modernity, and there are non-Christian philosophers who have attempted to flesh out a more postmodern approach to their discipline (e.g., Hilary Putnam). But now there also are *Christian* postmodernists who are expressing their views in a variety of subjects, such as philosophy, English, sociology, ethics, theology, and even youth ministry.

It is one thing for non-Christians to argue for a postmodern approach to understanding life, or their disciplines, but when Christians take this tack, much is at stake. If they are right, then, as Stanley Hauerwas asserts, the gospel is the true story but there is no way within history to prove it as such. We cannot know it is *really* true, for we cannot know objective truths. Instead, Christianity will be "true" merely because that is how we talk as Christians. That is, it is true because we say it is so.

That view, however, seems very different from the view of the apostle Paul. In Acts 17, he is addressing the men of Athens, and part of his claim is that God has given us evidence that Jesus is the true God:

> Therefore having overlooked the times of ignorance, God is now declaring to men that all everywhere should repent, because He has fixed a day in which He will judge the world in righteousness through a Man whom He has appointed, having furnished proof to all men by raising Him from the dead (Acts 17:30-31).

Paul says that God has indeed spoken, as a fact of reality, and that He is making a universally true claim: that all should repent, and that Jesus will judge them. And, most significantly, He actually has raised Jesus from the dead. For Paul, these are facts about the way things really are, and they are true for all people.

So we are faced with a fundamental conflict between postmodernism and Scripture. Nonetheless, Christian postmodernists try to persuade us that we too should see the world as they do. We now will turn to explore the specific views of some key Christian postmodernists, especially those of Stanley Hauerwas, Stanley Grenz, John Franke, and Brad Kallenberg. In so doing, not only will we see the specific ways postmodernism plays itself out in a Christian context, we will also be able to see more clearly the more general ideas of postmodernism.

"Theology, we might conclude, explores the world-constructing, knowledge-forming, identity-forming 'language' of the Christian community. But how does this relate to an objective reality beyond our linguistic constructs? . . . The simple fact is, we do not inhabit the 'world-in-itself'; instead, we live in a linguistic world of our own making."

STANLEY J. GRENZ AND JOHN R. FRANKE
BEYOND FOUNDATIONALISM, 53

T W O

WHAT IS *CHRISTIAN* POSTMODERNISM?

In this chapter, we will explore the specific ways postmodernism manifests itself in the works of four Christian writers. The first author is Stanley Hauerwas, who is perhaps the most prolific writer in ethics today and who writes as a theological ethicist. *Time* magazine honored him as America's foremost theologian in 2001. His works are studied in seminaries and Christian colleges as well as in secular religious studies programs. As two more examples, John Franke and the late Stanley Grenz are evangelical theologians and active contributors to the Evangelical Theological Society's meetings. Grenz has written voluminously, and much of his work focuses on revising evangelical theology on a more postmodern understanding. Finally, Brad Kallenberg is an evangelical philosophical theologian. He shares with Hauerwas many interests in Christian ethics. Like myself, he was on staff with a major Christian ministry for many years, and he was a member with me at Trinity Evangelical Free Church in Southern California. He studied at Fuller Seminary under Nancey Murphy, whose views also have influenced Tony Jones, the author of *Postmodern Youth Ministry* and a leader of the Emerging Church. Jones explicitly gives Murphy the credit for his understanding of postmodernism. In chapter 3, we will study Jones's views, along with those of Brian McLaren, another leader of the Emerging Church.

Besides discovering Hauerwas, Kallenberg, Grenz, and Franke's main ideas for a postmodern understanding of Christianity, we also will clarify more general traits of postmodernism. Let us begin, however, by drawing some analogies by which we may begin to understand what postmodernists are trying to say.

A FEW EXAMPLES

All of us are familiar with various fictional stories, whether written or in movies or plays. Authors create a "world" that may be very much like the real one, and realistic portrayals of characters, their situations, and their choices help draw us into their "world." But it is plain to us as the readers or viewers that this is just a story, one that the author has made through his or her words, and that we do not live in that world but in the real one.

Now suppose we are playing a computer game, such as "Sim City," the popular game in which various players can construct a town or city with the tools of the game, such as office buildings, homes, roads, and much, much more. In a sense, the players construct their "world," although again it is very obvious that this "world" is just that of a game; it obviously is not the same as the one in which we live.

Imagine now that you are a crew member of the starship *Enterprise*, with Captain Picard, Commander Riker, and the rest. Along with a few others, you need to go to the holodeck in order to simulate conditions in an old western town in nineteenth-century America. You instruct the computer to create this image, and you and your shipmates then enter into the scene. You have constructed this "world" by the commands you verbally gave to the computer, and in turn it simply followed its programming, which had been written (or spoken) by other persons before you.

In this "world," something goes wrong. You find that the bullets fired by the cowboys in a gunfight are real and deadly. You realize that somehow, the "game" has gone awry. Furthermore, you cannot get out of the program. You cannot escape and get back on board the *Enterprise*. Yet you still realize that there is a real world out there, which you have known as it is. Now, however, you just cannot get to it. Postmodernism is like this example in that we are on the "inside" of our language, as you are on the inside of the holodeck's program. But, unlike in the world as postmodernists describe it, we (assuming this *Star Trek* example) have known the real world as it truly, objectively is.

As another illustration, consider the movie *The Matrix*. Imagine that you, along with others, are characters inside the world created by the program in the movie. Imagine further that by becoming proficient in behaving according to the rules of the program, you can actually build, or make, your own world within this overall program. However, though you know there is a real world that exists apart from the program, you cannot get outside the program and know what that real world is actually like.

As with the other illustrations, postmodernism has similarities to (but is not exactly the same as) the ideas in *The Matrix.* Postmodernists say things like, "We cannot know objective reality." Yet, we all live in a "world" that has many different features, including legal, moral, political, social, religious, and other aspects. How do these come about? Together with others in our community, say the postmodernists, we build (or make, or shape, or construct) our worlds by how we talk and live, all of which is done by following the rules of our language. This aspect of postmodernism would be like the world we would build in *The Matrix* according to the rules of the program. And, the movie's program would be similar to the role of language in postmodernism. Let's now try to unpack the views of the Christian ethicists Hauerwas and Kallenberg, and then of the theologians Grenz and Franke, to see how they explain and understand their postmodern views.

HAUERWAS AND KALLENBERG

For Hauerwas and Kallenberg, much of the contemporary focus in ethics is misguided. Both think that the Enlightenment's effects upon ethics have been disastrous. Many Enlightenment philosophers thought that we could use our reason to know objective, universal truths. As we have seen already, Kant strongly held to this idea. The focus of his ethics, as well as that of most Enlightenment philosophers, is on the autonomous individual who through human reason can know moral truths, and from there the emphasis becomes how we are to make decisions in certain cases.

But one of the central issues that Hauerwas and Kallenberg raise against this view is that it tends to treat persons as something abstracted from the context in which they live and act. Furthermore, Hauerwas thinks that decision making as the focus of the moral life is very inadequate, for it overlooks the importance of the formation of our characters. For him, the moral life is cheapened when we treat it just as making right or wrong decisions; rather, it primarily must involve the development of our character.[1]

For Hauerwas and Kallenberg, the moral life is more than just making decisions; more importantly, it is one of *vision*, by which we see the moral truths found in a particular community. To have vision is to see moral truths, character qualities, situations, people, and the world rightly, so that we may act appropriately. To have a vision, though, requires stories, which are ways of connecting what we know about ourselves with the unknowns of the world.[2]

How then do we develop a moral vision, and which one do we choose? Importantly, for Hauerwas, there is no realm of facts that are just "out there," independent of how we characterize them. We must learn how to properly characterize and "see" the world, and we learn these characterizations, or descriptions, by learning the *language* of a community.[3] Kallenberg echoes this same idea, for as he claims, there simply is no way to get "outside" of the influence of language to know the real world as it actually is. We cultivate a moral vision by learning how to see the world, and this must be from a certain "aspect," or point of view. Learning how to perceive things "rightly" requires learning the ways a particular community (which for Hauerwas and Kallenberg is the church) describes the "world" from its point of view.

As with learning any language, we must learn the various expressions and when it is appropriate to use them. For example, when learning Spanish, I had to learn when it is appropriate to use the word *usted* versus *tú*. Both mean "you" in English, but the former is more formal and used usually with one's elders, while *tú* often is used with one's peers. Yet, in certain Spanish-speaking countries, they tend not to emphasize the use of the formal *usted* and just use *tú*. So you have to learn which terms are used in which kinds of contexts, and merely learning the grammatical rules may not be sufficient for learning how these words are used in a specific context.

In similar fashion, Hauerwas and Kallenberg emphasize the impor-

---

[1] Stanley Hauerwas and David B. Burrell, *Truthfulness and Tragedy* (Notre Dame, Ind.: University of Notre Dame Press, 1977), 20.
[2] Stanley Hauerwas, *Vision and Virtue* (Notre Dame, Ind.: Fides, 1974; reprint, Notre Dame, Ind.: University of Notre Dame Press, 1981), 71.
[3] Ibid., 20.

tance of learning the language of a given community in order to really understand and see how that community sees the world. Christians, they say, are those who have learned the language of the church, which, they say, is the Gospels, or more generally the Scriptures. The Bible is the authoritative source for how Christians should talk and live their lives, and more importantly, how they need to describe the world rightly, so that they may see it rightly.[4] As Hauerwas puts it, "we do not come to know the world by perceiving it [i.e., just going out and looking at it], but we come to know the world as we learn to use our language."[5]

Now in some respects these ideas may not seem unique. After all, Christians learn to see certain actions or attitudes as being sinful and not just as bad habits or something similar. And when we tell the gospel to others, we will explain that God loves us; our sins have separated us from God, who is holy; Jesus died for our sins and rose from the dead; and we can be born again if we receive Him as our Savior and Lord. So there are many terms the biblical writers use to explain the gospel and our human condition, and as believers, when we learn that what the Bible says is so, we learn to see ourselves and the world as they really are.

In itself, that is fine. But as I already have mentioned, Hauerwas and Kallenberg take this idea at least one step further. According to their view, there simply is no way we can know how things really (i.e., objectively) are. We cannot escape from the influences of language and somehow get "out" and know reality as it is apart from language. Instead, we need to learn how to see and live from the point of view of a certain community, and that requires learning its language.

However, where things get a bit tricky with this view is that Christians *do* have the truth. Throughout, the Bible clearly states what the truth is. For instance, Jesus said that He is the way, the truth, and the life, and that no one comes to the Father, but through Him (John 14:6). This is a bold claim, that salvation is found in no one else and is found exclusively in Jesus (see also Acts 4:12).

Herein lies the key issue: Since, according to these postmodernists, there is no way we can get "outside" of language and its pervasive influ-

---

[4] Stanley Hauerwas, *A Community of Character* (Notre Dame, Ind.: University of Notre Dame Press, 1981), 96.
[5] Hauerwas, *Vision and Virtue*, 71.

ence and know the real world, we "make" our worlds by how we talk. And this is what Hauerwas and Kallenberg tell us is the case. Kallenberg puts it quite bluntly: "Language does not represent reality, it constitutes reality."[6] Later we will see that Grenz and Franke believe much the same. So the Christian worldview, including its theological truth claims, is something that Christians make by how they use their language.

Before I continue to develop their views, let us try first to understand this concept of being "inside" language, and being unable to get "outside" of it. It does *not* mean that somehow language stands between us and the world. Rather, it is an epistemological idea that the effects of language are so pervasive that we cannot escape their influences on our thoughts, beliefs, and even experiences. (Instead of appealing to language, some people suggest that our *cultures* have this pervasive, inescapable influence on us. For our postmodern authors, though, language and culture are inseparable.)

We will see in the next chapter how Brian McLaren and Tony Jones think that we simply cannot achieve a neutral viewpoint from which we can know reality. This idea is very similar to that of Kallenberg, Hauerwas, Grenz, and Franke. For Kallenberg, there simply is no non-linguistic place to stand.[7] Here is another way Kallenberg expresses this concept, in a discussion of one aspect of Hauerwas's ethics:

> Ethics has an aesthetic component because of the givenness of language and narrative. We are each recipients of a communal way of life, of a stock of stories, of a conceptual vocabulary, and of a history of conversation; against these linguistic stones the lens of our moral vision is being ground. And we cannot put off our spectacles. For without them we are not only blind to our past responsibilities and myopic about our future; without them there is no "we" at all.[8]

To be "inside" language, as I use the term, is to be unable, as Kallenberg puts it, to even take off our "spectacles." It is to say that though there is a real world, our only way of knowing it is by our lan-

---

[6] Brad J. Kallenberg, *Ethics as Grammar: Changing the Postmodern Subject* (Notre Dame, Ind.: University of Notre Dame Press, 2001), 234.
[7] Ibid., 182.
[8] Ibid., 82.

guage use. To put this idea differently and more broadly, we cannot experience reality directly. Our experiences necessarily involve interpretations, a view I will address specifically in chapter 9. But there is an important extension of this concept, one which Kallenberg hints at in his last sentence in the quote above. Somehow, even who we are is integrally tied to our language. Language cannot be "pried off" from us, nor from the rest of the world we live in. They are inseparable; language and world are what they are in light of each other. That is, they are "internally related," to use Kallenberg's terms.[9]

But not just any old use of language will do, say Hauerwas and Kallenberg; Christians must learn how to conform their lives (and way of living) to the gospel. This involves primarily learning how to both talk and behave in the ways that the Gospels would require. Importantly, the *story* of Jesus is the normative standard, or goal, of the Christian life, and our stories should reflect His life and teachings. This is something that must take place in the Christian community with other Christians, who can help check up on the behavior (both verbal and nonverbal) of each other.[10]

Now, as we already have seen, it surely is true in the New Testament that Jesus Christ is the *telos,* or goal, of the Christian life. And we do indeed need other believers to help us grow into His likeness. But Hauerwas and Kallenberg have another reason for appealing to the importance of community, one more in keeping with their views of language. They believe that it is possible for us to truly live out the Christian life since, as humans, we are able to follow rules. It is the appropriate use of Christian language, within the Christian community, that enables us to truly live out the Christian life. Proper usage means that we have learned and now follow the "grammar" of the Christian language. We learn to describe our actions in terms of Christian words, such as "repenting," "forgiving," "witnessing," and so on. According to their view, we need our fellow community members to check up on our use of language, to correct us if we do not accurately use it.

At one level this is fine, for we do indeed learn to see our lives in

---

[9] Ibid., 184-192.
[10] See also my discussion in my *Virtue Ethics and Moral Knowledge: Philosophy of Language After MacIntyre and Hauerwas* (Aldershot, England: Ashgate, 2003), 76.

light of these and other Christian concepts. But Hauerwas and Kallenberg do not mean simply that we can accurately describe our lives, others, or the world as they really are (i.e., objectively). Rather, it is the very act of description that shapes and *makes* something into what it is. Thus, there is not some self that we may know as it really is. What, then, grounds our identity as particular individuals? According to their view, the soul is not the basis for our identity, for the soul is something that would exist as it is *apart* from language use. But, according to their view, that kind of move is ruled out, since we cannot get outside of language and know such things as they are.[11] Instead, what makes up a self is the *narrative,* or story, which that "character" lives out.[12]

Hauerwas and Kallenberg describe various "practices" that enable us to live out the Christian life and thereby become conformed to the "story" of Jesus. These practices include things such as prayer, works of mercy, worship, and witness. Let's look at the practice of witness, as it would be on their view. In traditional, evidential apologetics, we learn how to give arguments for God's existence, such as the cosmological argument or the design family of arguments. We also learn to defend the resurrection against biblical critics and skeptics. Hauerwas and Kallenberg would tell us, however, that all these attempts are misguided. Giving such arguments presupposes that we can know how things really are, that somehow we can escape language and get a "God's-eye view" of reality. But while we have that view in one sense (since God has given us special revelation in the Bible), it is a mistake to think we can give such arguments to people who are "inside" their own language. So Hauerwas argues that though the gospel is the true story, there still is no way within history to prove it as such. However, that doesn't mean that we cannot witness to nonbelievers. While there is no way to get past the influence of language and know reality (and be able to *say* how it really is), we can *show* the truth of the gospel by how we live in the Christian community. Hauerwas and Kallenberg argue that we must adopt an *embodied apologetic;* we must live out consistently the gospel

---

[11] Incidentally, some Christian postmodernists deny that the soul is a real entity. For Nancey Murphy, the soul is a "higher level" of description of the physical reality of our being. See her work in Warren S. Brown, Nancey Murphy, and H. Newton Malony, eds., *Whatever Happened to the Soul?* (Minneapolis: Fortress, 1998), e.g., 10, 139.

[12] Hauerwas, *A Community of Character,* 144.

story, and in that way we can show nonbelievers the truth of our faith. We encourage them to "come and see" the truth of our story by "trying on" the Christian way of life—by learning how we, members of the Christian community, live, talk, and behave. That is, by becoming an insider in our community, they can learn to see the truth of our faith, even though they never could know its veracity from the outside.[13]

If we cannot know reality as it is, but only by how we talk about it, then truth is not a matter of matching up (or corresponding) with reality. Instead it is a feature of the lives of Christians who faithfully live out the gospel story. So how do we learn to see the world "rightly," if we cannot know objective reality? We do this by the cultivation of skill in the Christian way of life. Accordingly Hauerwas wants to perform an ethical therapy in our lives, so that our stories are more in conformity with the story of Jesus. Such skill happens as we learn the language and behavior appropriate for the Christian community, and he and Kallenberg believe this will enable us to see the truthfulness of the Christian story.

Seeing the truth of the Christian story does not come about by gaining some neutral vantage point from which we supposedly can know objective truths, according to Hauerwas and Kallenberg. They think such an idea is an Enlightenment fiction. As Hauerwas puts it, there is no story of stories, no "metastory" or metanarrative that enables us to judge all other stories as either true or false.[14] Instead, it is training *within* the Christian way of life that enables us to see the truth of its story. So the most important kind of witness the church can provide to non-Christians is the creation of a living, breathing community of faith in which its members really live out consistently the story of Jesus.

Similarly, salvation is not some choice we make to accept Jesus into our lives.[15] That kind of understanding is based on the mistaken idea that we can know the objective truth about religion, and then can make a decision for Jesus (as opposed to some other religion or way of life). That kind of approach is one assumed by tracts such as *The Four Spiritual Laws*. But as we have seen, that idea is a mistake, according to their view. Salvation is not a matter of our standing outside of all ways

---

[13] Stanley Hauerwas and William H. Willimon, *Resident Aliens* (Nashville: Abingdon, 1989), 46-47.
[14] Hauerwas, *Community of Character*, 96.
[15] Kallenberg, *Ethics as Grammar*, 150.

of life and their languages, and then somehow seeing which one is objectively right. Rather, it is a process of being "engrafted" into the practices of the Christian community, such as witnessing, prayer, worship, and fellowship.[16] Again, all these practices are fundamentally matters of behaving according to the way the gospel says we should behave.

At this point it may seem that surely Hauerwas and Kallenberg's views are nothing but a dressed-up version of relativism. And on their face, their views *seem* relativistic. But Kallenberg has a key rebuttal against this charge. For him, to make the charge of relativism presupposes that someone can somehow get a neutral vantage point and see each community's languages and ways of living, and then somehow see that the truth *really* is that everything is relative to each community. But then he has a ready counter. That assumption, he says, is just an Enlightenment fiction, and it makes the same old mistake: that we can get outside language and see what is the objective truth (namely, that all is relative to each community). But we can never do that, he claims; we are always working from "within" language, and we cannot get "out." So this charge of relativism is just a claim made from within some particular community (one influenced by modern, Enlightenment thought), and that is *all* it is. Those who make the charge perpetuate the same old confusion when they think they can escape language and know the objective truth of the matter.[17]

GRENZ AND FRANKE

The evangelical theologians Stanley Grenz and John Franke offer a view very similar to that of Hauerwas and Kallenberg in their understanding of the role of language for Christian ethics and theology. In their book *Beyond Foundationalism,* Grenz and Franke lay out the contours of a more postmodern approach to Christian theology.[18] They believe such an approach is very much needed because we live in a time in which we no longer can believe that we can stand in some neutral vantage point and know reality. They assert that foundationalism, a view in philoso-

---

[16] Stanley Hauerwas, *In Good Company: The Church as Polis* (Notre Dame, Ind.: University of Notre Dame Press, 1995), 8.

[17] See Kallenberg, *Ethics as Grammar,* 227-250.

[18] Stanley Grenz and John Franke, *Beyond Foundationalism: Shaping Theology in a Postmodern Context* (Louisville: Westminster/John Knox, 2001).

phy that we can build our beliefs on a set of "foundational," basic beliefs that give us a connection with reality, is a dead position, a holdover from the Enlightenment.[19] On the contrary, they believe that "we do not inhabit the 'world-in-itself'; instead, we live in a linguistic world of our own making."[20] Further, they do not believe that we can escape from our particular social context and achieve a "transcultural intellectual vantage point."[21]

Why do they hold these beliefs? For Grenz and Franke, we never can know reality as it is. All our experiences are filtered through an "interpretative grid," which for them is fundamentally linguistic. Our language filters, conditions, and forms all our experience. In the case of Christians, it is Christian language, which is based on Scripture, which should be the focus of theology. As they put it, theology becomes the exploration of "the world-constructing, knowledge-forming, identity-forming 'language' of the Christian community."[22]

The relationship between language and the world in which we live is such that it seems we cannot get "outside" language and know objective truths. Drawing upon this insight, they insist on the local character of all theological reflection. That is, if we cannot get outside of language and have a universal, objective vantage point, then all theology must be the reflections of local Christian communities.[23] Furthermore, if there is no essence or nature to Christian language, then there are only the languages that are written and spoken in the various Christian communities around the world and down through time.

Even so, Grenz and Franke do not believe that we cannot ever know objective reality. They think there are three key ways we have a "hook" onto reality. The first is that the need to construct reality cannot extend to all of creation. As they observe, surely the universe existed before we came along. But that point does not do much work for them, for they hasten to mention that we live in a linguistically formed world of our own making.[24] Second, there is a sense in which Christians can know

---

[19] Ibid., 38.
[20] Ibid., 53.
[21] Ibid., 151.
[22] Ibid., 53.
[23] Ibid., 25; see also 166.
[24] Ibid.

the world as God wills it to be in the future, a view they call *eschato-logical realism*. That is, there is a plan God has revealed in Scripture about the way His kingdom will be when it is fully realized.

Third, and probably most important, Grenz and Franke maintain a way to know reality by believing that the Holy Spirit speaks to each Christian community today. That is, God is participating in our language games with us. In this way, the Spirit also is building the new community, the church. This move is highly significant, for it allows Grenz and Franke to think they have a way to gain an objective viewpoint, through God's "in-breaking" through our language, when we cannot get beyond the influences of language ourselves. God reveals reality to us in this way, so that Christians have the objective truth given to us by God, even though we ourselves could never get "outside" of language. The Holy Spirit is thereby able to unite the various individual Christian communities by working in each one's own specific historical context.

SUMMARY

Having completed our survey of the most relevant views of Hauerwas, Kallenberg, Grenz, and Franke, let us pause before moving on and summarize their key ideas. First, all four of these Christian authors think they have found the truth, or better, the true story, which is the story of Jesus. Second, though they maintain that Christians have the truth, they say that we are not able to know objective truth. This is because we are on the "inside" of language and cannot get "outside" of it to know the way reality objectively is. But instead of leaving us in a point of despair, Grenz and Franke are quite confident that while we cannot escape our language, God has been able to reveal the truth through His Spirit and special revelation.

Third, an implication of their views is that, since we cannot know the essential nature of things (since we are on the "inside" of language), we cannot know even an essence of language (or Christian language). Hence, there is not some universal thing known as Christian language; rather, there are just many discrete, unique Christian languages, each of which is tied to a local Christian community. Yet these unique Christian languages are united by a commitment to the gospel, which is the story of Jesus.

Fourth, as we saw in Hauerwas and Kallenberg, the emphasis in the Christian life should be on our stories becoming more and more like that of Jesus. We need to resist the temptation to offer apologetical arguments (at least, evidential ones) to non-Christians to help them see the truth of the gospel. That is a mistake, since truth (of the gospel, and of other matters) is not knowable apart from becoming a member of a community. And, the Holy Spirit reveals the truth of the story of Jesus in and through the Christian community. Thus, the most effective (and maybe the only kind of) witness Christians can give to outsiders is embodying and living out the story of Jesus in all that they do. This will enable outsiders to "see" the "truth" of the gospel and thereby enable them to become members of the Christian community.

So far we have surveyed these basic philosophical and more theoretical ideas in four postmodern Christian authors. Yet the influence of postmodernism is far broader than just in the theoretical arena. Leaders of the Emerging Church, such as pastors Brian McLaren and Tony Jones, pay attention to the cultural effects of modernity upon the church. They have their own suggestions for how ministry (as well as the faith itself) should be reorganized along postmodern lines. In chapter 3, we will survey their core ideas. Then in chapter 4 I will examine how postmodernism is at work in various disciplines in the secular and Christian universities.

"The post-evangelicals among us—and they are among us, in large numbers—are for the most part those who, because *of their evangelical insights or suspicions, cannot accept a* form of *evangelical religious culture that makes the heart of the evangelical faith irrelevant and the heart of the prophetic biblical tradition anything but subversive. We need to listen to them openly and carefully as we continue to study our Bibles and seek to hear from God."*

DALLAS WILLARD, FOREWORD TO *THE POST-EVANGELICAL*
BY DAVE TOMLINSON, REVISED NORTH AMERICAN EDITION

THREE

THE EMERGING CHURCH

Postmodernism in general, and Christian postmodernism in particular, is not just a set of philosophical beliefs, although those are very important. It also is a cultural shift, a kind of mind-set that has its own characteristics, as well as a response to modernity. Likewise, modernity (or, the Enlightenment project) is more than just a set of philosophical views. It too has its own kinds of cultural effects, which have had a profound impact on the way we live, think, and feel, both in the broader Western culture and specifically within the church.

I think that key leaders within the "Emerging Church" are looking at these kinds of issues closely. In this chapter, I want to look carefully at the views of two such people. First is Brian McLaren, who perhaps is the most widely read author in the field. As a pastor who has made his own transition through a crisis from a modern mind-set to a postmodern one, McLaren offers perhaps the most carefully nuanced, thoughtful viewpoints on the practical effects of modernity upon the church. I think there is much we can learn from him, so I will devote much of this chapter to an exposition of his main ideas.

In addition, I want to look carefully at the views and suggestions offered by a second leader in the Emerging Church, Tony Jones. Arguably, our youth today have been growing up in a postmodern setting, or at least in a culture strongly influenced by postmodern thought. We should expect, therefore, that postmodernism would be impacting how youth ministry is being done, and that is what we find. In *Postmodern Youth Ministry*,[1] which was published by Youth Specialties,

---

[1] Tony Jones, *Postmodern Youth Ministry* (Grand Rapids, Mich.: Zondervan/Youth Specialties, 2001). I am finding that Youth Specialties is providing much material on doing ministry in a postmodern context, and it also sponsored Brian McLaren's "open letter" to Charles Colson, in response to Colson's brief, critical essay on postmodernism in *Christianity Today*. For more on Youth Specialties, and in particular the McLaren letter, see www.youthspecialties.com/articles/topics/postmodernism/open_letter.php. For Colson's original essay, see "The Postmodern Crackup: From Soccer Moms to College Campuses, Signs of the End," *Christianity Today* (December 2003), 72.

Jones advocates that youth workers need to start looking at the Bible through the same kind of eyes that their students have been born with, namely, postmodern ones. In order not to let another significant cultural watershed pass by the church, he argues that youth ministers need to be careful students of culture, which he says is largely postmodern.[2] But beyond mere understanding of the postmodern mind-set of today's students, Jones also argues that faith itself needs to be reconceived along certain postmodern lines of thought, which he has become aware of mainly from his studies at Fuller Seminary under Nancey Murphy.[3]

In this chapter, we will look at the more practical effects of modernity on the broader culture and on the church, from the viewpoints of McLaren and Jones. Then we will examine the ways these two leaders of the Emerging Church conceive of the practice of our faith in ways that incorporate key insights of postmodernism. Indeed, McLaren and Jones think that not only can we help people's faith survive in a postmodern world; it can *thrive* in such times.[4] This chapter will not assess their views so much as try to accurately represent them.[5] The next chapter will look at how postmodernism is at work in the university, and the following chapters will evaluate postmodernism and the Emerging Church.

BRIAN MCLAREN

In his award-winning book *A New Kind of Christian*, Brian McLaren prefaces his tale of Dan Poole and Neil Edward Oliver ("Neo") with a few insights into his own story. As he tells it, he had been teaching English at the college level, and he had been pastoring in an evangelical church for a number of years. Then, over time, several factors combined to precipitate a crisis in his life, especially in his faith, such that he got to the point where he was sick of being a pastor, and even contemplated giving up the faith.

What had brought on this crisis? One factor was an expectation that he felt he could no longer live with in good conscience—the expectation

---

[2] Jones, *Postmodern Youth Ministry*, 38.
[3] Ibid., 8.
[4] Ibid., 12.
[5] I will focus on three of McLaren's books: *A New Kind of Christian* (San Francisco: Jossey-Bass, 2001); *The Story We Find Ourselves In* (San Francisco: Jossey-Bass, 2003); and *More Ready Than You Realize* (Grand Rapids, Mich.: Zondervan, 2002).

that pastors should have absolute certainty in their faith, with "bombproof" answers to tough questions. Another was the view, and expectation, that the gospel could be "reduced" to four laws or a few simple steps to have peace with God, and that the Christian life could be explained by a set of easy steps to follow. McLaren came to believe that life itself is not that simple, and nothing is that sure. Indeed, he found that in a church where he was trying to minister to both "veterans" of the church and seekers, these formulas sounded good to the saved but utterly weird to the seekers. It seemed to him that Christianity, at least as ordinarily conceived, had no new insights to offer people besides these stock formulas, which made the situations much worse when they confronted hard realities in life. Plus, when he would try to preach a sermon designed to reach the seekers, he would receive critical comments from the "vets." It seemed that he could please one group but not the other.

But there were more factors leading to McLaren's crisis. One was that he saw how little difference the gospel was making in the lives of believers. That is, too many were living very inauthentically as Christians, often being quite proud, rather than humble servants. He also believed that no one theological system could account for all biblical passages.

So it seems that McLaren's expectations, which were fed and reinforced by a particular conception, or "framework," of the faith, helped land him in a crisis when these challenges arose. To keep on being a Christian in that same old way would simply perpetuate his crisis. But he also indicates that he resonated with comments some people would make about changes at work in the Industrial Age, and that our Industrial Age faith would change too. He also met some people who modeled for him what a "new kind" of Christian might look like. So, there was hope. He wouldn't need to give up Christianity or even the pastorate; he merely needed to give up his way of thinking and expectations as to how a Christian should live, think, and feel.

McLaren's chosen genre for communicating his ideas in two key books is narrative, which fits well with a postmodern approach. In *A New Kind of Christian*, as well as its sequel, *The Story We Find Ourselves In*, he uses characters such as Dan, an evangelical pastor who is facing a crisis similar to McLaren's own, and Neo, who already has made the transition from being a modern Christian to being a post-modern one. McLaren is careful to point out that we, his readers, should be careful not to attribute to him these characters' specific views, which makes it more challenging to identify McLaren's own views. Nonetheless, there are themes that keep emerging, and McLaren uses these characters and the plot to communicate several key ideas for his readers about modernity and its influences, and how a new, postmodern kind of Christian might live and see the world.

Modernity's Cultural Influences

Throughout these books, as well as in a third book, *More Ready Than You Realize,* McLaren highlights several broad attitudes and cultural effects of modernity, especially upon the broader culture, which in turn have had their ramifications in the way Christians perceive how they should understand and live out their faith. I will consider his account of the effects upon our broader culture before looking at specific influences on the church.

In *A New Kind of Christian,* McLaren, through Neo, tells us about several main attitudes and expectations that characterize a modern way of thinking.[6] The first, he says, is a desire to *control and conquer,* which is reflected in our drives to master our world technologically and scientifically. Philosophically, we have sought to build all-encompassing systems that would explain everything, thereby taking the mystery out of life (and faith). This same drive has manifested itself in imperialistic endeavors abroad, and economically, in people's efforts to dominate markets.

Second, McLaren observes that the modern era can be characterized as *the age of the machine.* In this worldview, we see the world, and people, too, as mechanisms, which can be programmed, controlled, and broken down or "reduced" to their smallest units. They are subject to complete scientific explanation and mastery. Third, the modern era is *the age of analysis,* in which that form of thought has become regarded as ultimate. This way of thinking has led us to try to find neat, systematic categories into which to fit all knowledge. By seeing the universe as a machine, science has become the "master screwdriver" that can take it

---

[6] McLaren, *A New Kind of Christian,* 16-18.

apart, bit by bit, to unlock all its secrets. But it is not just any kind of science; it is *secular* science, which is the fourth trait of modernity.

Fifth, modernity has been marked by a *quest for certainty and absolute, "totalizing" knowledge*. This is similar to what we observed above, that in the modern period people have searched for a grand theory of "everything." Our theoretical beliefs should attempt to explain all aspects of life and existence. Often people think science is the discipline that can unlock all mysteries, particularly by use of the scientific method. But here, McLaren also calls our attention to further attitudes. It is the quest to find certain knowledge, based on indubitable foundations. That is, how we provide support for our beliefs is like a building: it must rest upon a solid, secure foundation; and in terms of our knowledge, that foundation must be certain, so that we cannot possibly doubt it. This is McLaren's understanding of the epistemological view known as *foundationalism,*[7] a view that Jones also will address and criticize.

Sixth, modernity is a *critical age,* in that if you know truth with absolute certainty, then you must debunk any who see things differently. Seventh, it is the age of the *modern nation-state,* as well as large-scale, global organizations. Eighth, modernity is marked by great attention on me, *the individual,* whether that is in terms of morality, salvation and worship, marketing ads, or many other aspects of life. Ninth, *Protestantism* characterizes modernity, and tenth, so does widespread *consumerism.*

In summary, these are McLaren's main observations about modernity's general traits and effects upon our broader culture. He then goes on to make some very thought-provoking comments about the extent to which the church has been influenced by these same attitudes and expectations. It is here, I think, that McLaren poses questions and concerns that we as believers must ponder and carefully assess, as we live in a culture that has been very shaped by modern thought and values and that now is being influenced by postmodern ones.

---

[7] Later, however, I will argue against this portrait of foundationalism, for it is not the kind of foundationalism that most philosophers accept today. And, to require 100 percent, "bombproof" certainty will make knowledge vulnerable to skeptical attacks. Skeptics can readily counter, "But, isn't it just *possible* that you could be mistaken?" Now, it is hard to rule out completely any such possibility, so we answer yes, but then the skeptic has us where he or she wants us: "*If you can't be certain, then you can't know.*" But that is too high a standard for knowledge, as we will see.

Modernity's Influence on the Church

McLaren addresses the influences of modernity on the church in several places. In *More Ready Than You Realize,* McLaren gives a short list of such influences.[8] Just as modernity sought to conquer and control, whether that be through imperialistic efforts, technology, or the attempt to subjugate every aspect of life under science's dominion, so the church has tended to adopt similar attitudes and even *terminology.* For instance, he thinks the church exhibits this mind-set when we call our evangelistic efforts (or even organizations) "crusades," which implies the idea of a military invasion and conquest.

In evangelism, he says, we have often tended to reduce the gospel message to a simple tract, in which the whole message has been packaged as simple laws and steps.[9] Just as science supposedly has given us the absolute truth about the realm of nature and physical laws, so we have packaged the essential, absolute spiritual truths. But if that is the case, where is there any room for someone to discuss those laws with us? The person to whom we present these truths is left with the options of either accepting or rejecting them, with no room for discussion. This mind-set also treats people's questions, which may be rooted in profoundly difficult life experiences, as being subject to easy, simple answers.

We also talk about evangelism as "winning" people to Christ, but that implies that someone "loses." In that kind of view, McLaren thinks we tend to view evangelism as encounters that are aimed at trying to convert the person by winning an argument, as though rational acceptance of the truths as presented is all that is needed for the person to become a follower of Jesus. But in that approach, we often fail to really value a genuine friendship with a person, instead preferring to see our times together as times that must be aimed at winning that person to Jesus. In short, the methodology is *coercive, not loving.* In that process, our faith also tends to be treated as a rigid belief system that must be accepted, instead of a unique, joyful way of living, loving, and serving.[10]

In this kind of ethos, our apologetics naturally becomes a defense, which terminology also implies that there is a war going on, and thus

---

[8] McLaren, *More Ready Than You Realize,* 25.
[9] Tony Jones sees this as "a natural outgrowth of foundationalism; that is, foundationalism begets reductionism" (private e-mail correspondence, June 22, 2004).
[10] McLaren, *More Ready Than You Realize,* 41-42.

we tend not to pursue a friendship with people, to love them, whether or not they ever become Christ's disciples.[11] It also implies that we become *defensive,* a posture that indeed has often characterized believers in the face of the pressures and criticisms given by secular intellectuals and other such elite. In our apologetics, we try to give airtight, irrefutable arguments aimed to win the debate, but that puts us in a position from which we challenge others to prove us wrong while we prove to them that we are right. In that mind-set, we act as though we are in a court case, or a debate, where we must *make our case* and provide *evidence,* all of which is to lead up to *the verdict* that Christianity is absolutely true.[12] But, according to McLaren, that combative "I win, you lose" approach turns people off. In addition to valuing truth, postmodern people value authenticity in the way people follow particular religions. So, if we preach that God loves people, postmoderns want to see that our lives match our message. Instead, according to McLaren, what they often see is that Christians are angry, reacting against pressures and challenges posed by those who disagree with them.[13]

Furthermore, McLaren thinks that Christianity itself has come to be seen as mechanistic and deterministic.[14] In modernity, people have tried to pin everything down to nice, neat categories, by analyzing things down to their constitutive elements. McLaren thinks we have tended to treat God similarly. By thinking we can convey the whole truth of the gospel in simple laws and steps, and that we can understand our discipleship to Jesus in terms of simple concepts, we have tended to take away the mystery from who God is. We lose our sense of wonder and awe at who God is, and how great He is, as well as the joy and freedom that comes from living in a vital relationship with Him.[15]

The modern influences have tended to leave evangelicals with a view of God as controlling, rigid, and requiring utter certainty in our beliefs, which should be sufficient to dispel any heartfelt concerns or questions we may have in our walk with Him. If we have doubts, then there is

---

[11] Ibid., 48.

[12] Ibid., 148.

[13] For instance, see McLaren, *More Ready Than You Realize,* 158.

[14] Ibid., 116. See also McLaren, *The Story We Find Ourselves In,* 83, where Neo and Kerry discuss a modern view of God as controlling and manipulative. See also the passage in *More Ready Than You Realize,* 63-64, where McLaren discusses modern Christians' view of God as being uptight, rigid, and controlling.

[15] McLaren, *More Ready Than You Realize,* 148.

something wrong with us, which we should confess. The Christian life is a belief system, a transmission of information,[16] which we should accept fully; and if we have struggles, then it is a reflection upon us and our lack of faith or some other sin.

For McLaren, when we treat Christianity as a "belief system" that focuses on the transmission of certain, indubitable truths which are contained in Scripture, then we ought to be able to put all truths into neat and tidy categories, by using an analytical method. To a modern understanding, this is the goal of our systematic theologies: to impose an analytical outline on the Bible, to mine it for all truths and answers, which are absolutely true. This approach tends to view God as an engineer who has organized all truths in clean systems that can be logically understood.

Modernity has so influenced the church in these ways that we have tended to become arrogant and rigid, defensive and legalistic. According to McLaren, we have tended to react and become defensive when challenged by secular people's pressures; we try to keep our beliefs pure, safe, and sanitized, being afraid of heresy and wrong beliefs. We have tried to become powerful and "conquer" when political decisions have not gone our way, trying to impose our values on others, thinking that a coercive approach will be right and the way to please God. We have become arrogant in thinking that our system of belief is utterly true, so that we do not tend to love others if they do not believe our message. And we have become legalistic, in that we think we have the Christian life all figured out as a system of beliefs to be believed and obeyed, and if something doesn't work, it is the believer's own fault—not something wrong with the modern way of living out Christianity.

What are some more repercussions of modernism for the church itself? As you might imagine, there are several. As Christians, McLaren thinks we have given lip service to being a community of believers, when in actual practice we live like moderns—with an inordinate focus on Christians as *individuals*.[17] We have lost a deep sense of body life, so that when postmodern people are looking for authentic people, who love each other in community, the church generally just doesn't live up to its promise. We also become so focused on saving individuals' souls that we

---

[16] Ibid., 167.
[17] McLaren, *A New Kind of Christian*, 99.

neglect the role of the body of Christ in saving souls (such as in the example that Hauerwas gives, of our lives *being* an embodied apologetic).[18] This same focus on individuals results in an attitude that tends to forget the nations, social needs like justice, and care for the environment.[19]

Perhaps one of McLaren's most provocative comments about the influence of modernity on the church is his concern that though the church is here to serve, all too often it has become a purveyor of religious goods and services.[20] In modernity's consumeristic orientation, too often the church has competed for "market share" and "clientele," or customers, with all other businesses and organizations that vie for our attention and loyalties. But the church does not exist to satisfy the demands of believers. Instead, the church needs to be a community that is faithful to the Lord Jesus, believing and living out our faith as He would have us live. That is, the church is a community of people who are engaged in a mission, to help reconcile the entire world under Jesus as Lord.

Still, for McLaren, it is not so much that modernity is bad, and postmodernism is good, but rather it is a matter of what is appropriate versus inappropriate.[21] Modernity has influenced our view of the Christian life, the church, and how we as Christians are to relate to broader society in ways of which we are largely unconscious. But business-as-usual just will not help us reach postmoderns, and it also keeps us trapped in a modern approach to Christianity, which, he claims, is fading away.

The Postmodern Shift: The Changes in Our Cultural Mind-set

In what ways is modernity fading away? McLaren thinks that, for one, it is fading away in the mind-sets and attitudes among those who have been significantly shaped by postmodern thought. Postmoderns want genuine friendships, and they want to see that our lives really match up to our words. In short, they want to see that we are authentic. In evan-

---

[18] Ibid., 82.
[19] See McLaren, *A New Kind of Christian,* 73, where Neo discusses how we need to reconceive reconciliation in a holistic way.
[20] Ibid., 156.
[21] Ibid., 22.

gelism, that means they want to see that Christians genuinely care for them, and not just for the sake of seeing them convert to Christianity.

Closely related, they value community, and in our highly individualistic culture, this is a much-needed corrective. This takes a unique turn for postmoderns. In looking at churches, they want to find a place where they can belong *before* they have to believe.[22] McLaren wants our churches to be such places, where we serve one another, listen to and care for one another, where we truly live out the "one another" commands in Scripture.

Instead of being fixated on whether people are "saved" or "not saved," McLaren contends we should see conversion as a process, and our part in evangelism is to help encourage people in that process. When we try to pin people down into exact categories, to determine if they are "in" or "out" of the kingdom, we actually buy into modernity's emphasis to try to have everything understood and spelled out.[23] Instead of trying to get people to go through a simplified version of the gospel and pray a prayer, McLaren thinks we should learn from the methods of Jesus Himself, who was long on telling stories but short on sermons. He was short on abstractions but long on asking good questions. He also was short on telling us what to think but long on challenging us to think for ourselves. Yes, He did argue, says McLaren, but not from a superior, know-it-all position (as though that is what a modern approach to evangelism requires).[24]

Another "mind-set shift" McLaren observes is that postmoderns want to find wonder and mystery again in the world, and they are not content with modernity's attempts to explain everything, especially by science. A key way this plays out is in religion; McLaren says that postmoderns don't want a God who has been shrunken down to modern tastes.[25] If God does transcend us, then there ought to be aspects to our theology that truly reflect that belief, and we should not try to dissect God as if expecting to fully comprehend Him. Plus, our worship services should incorporate aspects of worship long since forgotten by modernity's emphasis on abstract reasoning. For example, various arts and

---

[22] McLaren, *More Ready Than You Realize*, 9, 84.
[23] Ibid., 101.
[24] E.g., McLaren, *More Ready Than You Realize*, 26-28.
[25] Ibid., 52.

imagery could be employed in the service, to help the worshipers grasp by way of their senses something of God's transcendence.

Also, these days, McLaren observes that people "are concerned about God's attitude toward contemporary women, minorities, and homosexuals."[26] They want to know if God is compassionate and just, or rigidly legalistic, like many Christians.

Thus far, I have surveyed key problems McLaren sees with modernity's influence on our culture and especially on the church. We also have looked at a few values and attitudes prevalent among postmoderns. While I think this is McLaren's emphasis, there are also philosophical issues he hints at in his works. I now will shift to survey his philosophical ideas, which in *A New Kind of Christian* and *The Story We Find Ourselves In* often are expressed in the words of his characters Dan or Neo. In the case of those two narratives, often we must infer just what are McLaren's own views. But elsewhere we may see what he believes from essays and interviews on his website,[27] and from *More Ready Than You Realize.*

The Postmodern Shift: The Philosophical Changes

In *A New Kind of Christian*, Neo explains to a Christian college group that postmodernism has "deconstructed" much of modern thought.[28] Here he examines the shifts from the medieval era to the modern era, and the modern to the postmodern. He catalogs seven key areas of major changes: (1) changes in communication technology, with major effects on how people think and live; (2) changes in our scientific worldview, with "staggering implications"; (3) the rise of a new intellectual elite that challenges authority and introduces a new epistemology; (4) changes in transportation technologies that increase our abilities to interact around the globe, thereby making the world seem smaller; (5) the decay and replacement of an older economic system with a newer one; (6) new military technology; and (7) new assaults on the current authorities, which in turn reply defensively.

But what is deconstructionism? Jacques Derrida (1930–2004) is

---

[26] Ibid., 71.
[27] See www.anewkindofchristian.com.
[28] McLaren, *A New Kind of Christian*, 29-31.

known as its founder, and its ideas are closely tied to the postmodern thought we have studied in the previous chapter. Writing well after the linguistic turn in philosophy, Derrida says that all meanings depend for their existence upon individual acts of language. These acts are constantly changing and thus so are our meanings. For Derrida, there always is *differance*, or, loosely translated, "difference," between any two uses of words. There are no two things that are exactly the same, even words, so meanings are always differing from one use of language to another. Furthermore, we the readers can break down the apparent, surface meaning of a text, and ask various questions and develop issues hidden in the text, such as, what hierarchical power relations are at work in the writing? Even more so, our interpretations do not enable us to get to the intended meaning of the author, as though that is something that exists in its own right. That would be something unchangeable, something that could not differ from use to use. Rather, our interpretations reveal key things about *us*, such as our privileged points of view, our biases, or our position of power. And, as Tony Jones has reminded me, "there is always more to the text than we can find,"[29] even when we try to pin down its meaning.

According to Neo, postmodern thinkers apparently have deconstructed and unmasked the modern quest for universal truth and certainty, and the attempt to dominate and control all aspects of life, and they have exposed these as being a will to power. Hence, modern claims to actually having achieved such knowledge of universal truth and other such goals are just a pretense. In this passage, Neo apparently thinks that the postmodern deconstructions of modernity have been quite apt, for he tells us that the choice for these students is between (a) being faithful to their Christian upbringing with all its modern trappings, which is fading away; or (b) venturing ahead in faith, to practice devotion in the new, "emerging culture of postmodernity."[30]

Many other lines of thought in McLaren's writings give some indication as to how he views postmodernism's key philosophical ideas. Instead of being able to gain a universal, ahistorical vantage point, as moderns seemed to seek, McLaren reminds us that all our perspectives

---

[29] Jones, private e-mail correspondence, June 22, 2004.
[30] McLaren, *A New Kind of Christian*, 38.

are just that—perspectives, from our own particular, cultural, historically situated places. Our viewpoints are limited and contingent, changing and not privileged.[31] Indeed, he claims that nothing is purely
objective, even our viewpoints, for all things have personal value and
meaning.[32] That is an interesting sense of the word "objective." As Jones
explains, McLaren seems to mean "'objective' as opposed to 'subjective',
and since we are each a subject, we necessarily view things subjectively."[33] That is, we all have our particular points of view. We are not
neutral or "objective," in a disinterested sense.

The contingency of our viewpoints has a corollary, according to
McLaren. If our viewpoints are contingent, then the Cartesian epistemological view of foundationalism (at least as he understands it), that
our beliefs are justified by their being supported by indubitable, certain,
"bombproof" beliefs in the "foundations," is wrong. By trying to build
our faith on a bedrock of absolutely certain beliefs (even from Scripture),
we face great problems when we encounter situations in life that defy
simple, absolute explanations. Instead, our beliefs are better understood
as being related to each other in a mosaic, or web, much as the philosopher W. V. O. Quine taught us.[34] Instead of basing our beliefs (and our
faith) on a misguided attempt to find utter certainty, when life stub-
bornly refuses such attempts, we need a better approach, one that has
many anchor points to reality, like a spider's web. Along these lines,
McLaren refers briefly to the sociologist Peter Berger's work, as well as
that of Grenz and Franke in theology, and he also refers us to the work
of Thomas Kuhn in philosophy of science.

In sharp contrast to the modern attitudes that we could find absolutely certain truths through universal human reason, postmodernism
instead stresses a humility of knowledge, which appeals to postmodern
people today. Repeatedly, certain knowledge is a theme McLaren returns
to as a hallmark of modernity and therefore as a prime reason to reject
modern ways of thinking. As we have seen, McLaren points out that life
is not so simple, and to think that we can have certainty in our inter-

---

[31] McLaren, *More Ready Than You Realize*, 76. According to him, our viewpoints aren't "privileged"
in that they do not afford us unique access to know universal truths.
[32] Ibid., 94.
[33] Jones, private e-mail correspondence, June 22, 2004.
[34] McLaren, *More Ready Than You Realize*, 129. Nancey Murphy also appeals to Quine's view of the
web of beliefs as her postmodern alternative to foundationalism.

pretations betrays the fact that we all have blind spots. An appeal to certain, unalterable truths lends itself to a rigid approach to the faith—the attitude that we must live, think, and feel in certain predefined ways. But that rigidity undercuts a central aspect of our message—that Christians are to live out their faith with great joy and love, as Jesus did.

In contrast to our having unhindered access to universal truth, which can lead to dogmatic attitudes, Christians, says McLaren, should be marked by humility, even in our knowledge claims. By rejecting the Enlightenment penchant for attaining to absolute truth through universal human reason, McLaren thinks that postmodernism makes room for faith. Otherwise, we think we have everything wired and figured out, by employing reason that is totalizing in its reach. With such an attitude, we tend to think we can completely figure out God. But the end result of such intellectual confidence is that, instead of standing in awe of God, who is ultimately beyond our ability to fully comprehend, we end up putting Him in a box.

There are other reasons why McLaren wants to move away from the belief that reason can attain to absolute truth. Not only does he believe that we all have blind spots and cannot have certainty in our interpretations, McLaren also claims that all truth is contextual.[35] No meanings can exist without context, he claims, and this is a major reason why he thinks that everything finds its meaning in its place in a story, or narrative. In modern Christianity, he claims, doctrines have been treated as free-floating abstractions that are true even apart from their context in the Christian story. It is as though we think the meaning of the Bible is available to anyone (again, because of the modern idea of universal reason). But, for McLaren, that is not so, for to understand anything we have to apprentice ourselves to a community. Hence, to understand Christian thought, people need to become part of the Christian community, so that they can see the truth of Scripture embodied in its people.[36]

Why is it so important to postmodernist Christians that people see truth from the vantage point of a community? In part, this is due to their view of the role of language. In various places, McLaren hints at the

---

[35] McLaren, *A New Kind of Christian,* 106.
[36] Ibid., 70.

importance of language for his views, yet he is not so clear as some of the other Christian postmoderns we read about in the previous chapter. Nonetheless, he has several things he wants to tell us about language. In *A New Kind of Christian*, Neo tells us that a huge part of who we are flows from language,[37] but then he does not clarify what that means. Does Neo mean our sense of our self-understanding, which we express in language? Or does he mean that language somehow constitutes reality, as Kallenberg says? Or does he mean something entirely different? In *The Story We Find Ourselves In*, Neo remarks that we are "stuck" in language.[38] Again, what does this mean? If it means that we work within the limitations of language (understood as verbal and nonverbal behaviors) to express our thoughts, feelings, desires, etc., to others, then that is easy enough to accept as true. But if it means what Kallenberg and others hold, that we are on the "inside" of language and cannot get beyond its influence to know objective reality, then we have a much stronger claim.

Perhaps we can get more illumination from other passages. Neo tells Dan that history began with our *ability to write history,*[39] as though events and the language used to describe them are inseparable. If this is so, then historical events are what they are in light of the language used to write history; they would not be what they are apart from the language used by an author to report and record them.

Neo also muses that it would be better to speak of the "language of creation" than of "natural laws."[40] For him, it is more fruitful to speak of the universe as poetry than as a machine (as modernity taught us). We are learning to see that the universe has possibilities and novelty, as well as information, and that new properties seem to emerge. This view stands opposed to seeing the universe as simply static and mechanical, as under the modern view. It does not make sense to Neo to think of the universe as having natural versus supernatural distinctions, for it "didn't come equipped with these categories."[41] Those are human constructions we have imposed on creation, instead of seeing it as God's creation, as

---

[37] Ibid., 100.
[38] McLaren, *The Story We Find Ourselves In*, 28.
[39] McLaren, *A New Kind of Christian*, 15.
[40] McLaren, *The Story We Find Ourselves In*, 43, 160.
[41] Ibid., 49.

a whole. It is as though the universe operates on many levels, capable of being described on many levels but yet capable of being a whole.[42] This view would counter the modern urge to dissect all that exists into their smallest constituent parts, treating them atomistically rather than as a whole.

Finally, Neo explains that though we all live on planet Earth, we still live in different universes, depending on the kind of God we believe in and our understanding of the master story of which we are a part.[43] Sometimes we may speak of living in completely different worlds, in that our experiences and cultures can be so radically different, like the differences I experienced between living in the United States and living in the Democratic Republic of the Congo, in Africa. But Neo doesn't say we live in different *understandings* of the same universe; he says we live in different *universes*. If McLaren thinks language and world are internally related, then such a comment reflects the ideas we have seen in Kallenberg, Hauerwas, Grenz, and Franke. And it does seem that McLaren thinks that we are what we are in light of our story(ies).

So McLaren's reasoning appears to be twofold. First, our culture is going postmodern, and to relate to postmoderns, we need to understand postmodern thought. That is a more descriptive claim, along with a key missiological insight—that we need to consider how we will contextualize the gospel to reach a people group (in this case, postmoderns). But there is also his second line of thought: that many believe postmodernism has *successfully* deconstructed modernism's main positions, and that therefore we *should* give up modernity's key ideas and we should develop new ways of thinking and talking about the Christian faith.[44] In some ways, this is a more implicit stance by McLaren, and it clearly is philosophical in nature. I say that it is implicit because Neo mentions more than once that there are philosophical figures at the fountainhead of postmodernism, thinkers such as Derrida, Michael Polanyi, Martin Heidegger, Nancey Murphy, and others (among whom are theologians, such as Grenz and Franke, and Lesslie Newbigin). What is interesting,

---

[42] See, e.g., McLaren, *The Story We Find Ourselves In*, 43. This account of levels of description reminds me of Nancey Murphy's concept in *Anglo-American Postmodernity* (Boulder, Colo.: Westview, 1997), chapter 10.

[43] McLaren, *A New Kind of Christian*, 161.

[44] I appreciate Tony Jones's helpful comments here on a first draft of this chapter in our e-mail correspondence on June 22, 2004.

I think, is that McLaren deflects the philosophical questions, choosing instead to voice through Neo that it is possible to describe broader culture without going too deeply into postmodern philosophy.[45] Neo says he can remain on a descriptive level without having to explain the philosophy of people like Michel Foucault, Richard Rorty, Stanley Fish, or others. Later we will return to this matter, to see if McLaren really can (or should) avoid a discussion of the philosophy behind postmodern thought and practice.

How to Be a New Kind of Christian

We already have explored many aspects of McLaren's positive views—that is, how we as Christians should live and think in light of postmodernism. Here I will summarize some of them. A major thrust is that we need to recast our theology in terms of being rooted in the Christian story, which is told in Scripture. We also need to see the truth of the faith not as a set of abstract propositions but as something that somehow cannot make sense apart from the story in which it has its meaning.

This, says McLaren, means that we should reconceive how we witness to people. It should not be the presentation of a set of abstract principles, or "laws," as though they make sense to anyone. Instead, the truth of the gospel makes sense in terms of the story of Jesus. Coupled with this idea is the idea that postmodern people want to see the truth of our faith by how we live it out in community. They need to see the authentic Jesus in our midst, that we embody the truth of the faith in our "truthful" lives (as Hauerwas would say).

So evangelism becomes more of a dance, a kind of movement back and forth, in the context of a friendship that is done for the sake of really valuing the person, and not merely for the sake of "winning" the person to Christ. McLaren therefore sees our churches as places where people can belong *before* they believe. Evangelism is not to be done from a "superior" position as if we know it all, but instead it is to be done as a conversation, in which we listen and genuinely care for people, telling the story of Jesus as well as our own story of our relationship with Him.

---

[45] McLaren, *A New Kind of Christian*, 19.

If we put our focus on the story of Jesus, while others have their stories, is there a place for rationality and logic in evangelism, as well as in the rest of church life? McLaren definitely affirms that the gospel should be logical and rational, but we should not use logic or arguments in a way to "win" the person, thereby implying that someone loses.[46] He does not say that there is no place for propositional truth in evangelism, but we need to share our stories, for it is in these stories that propositions have their meaning and proper place, or context.[47] Also, we need to resist the modern urge to subsume our faith under a "totalizing," rational system (e.g., a systematic theology with such pretensions) that in effect removes all mystery from the Christian faith. There must be room for faith, and we cannot reduce God down to our level.

In short, McLaren advocates that the church needs to be a place where its members are real and down to earth, closely interweaving theory and practice, so that we truly embody the faith. Yes, the faith needs to be rational, true, and credible, but it also must be authentic, powerful, and able to redeem lives, demonstrate reconciliation, and build a community in which its people live as authentic followers of Jesus. The modern challenge was to prove our faith right and other religions wrong, but the postmodern challenge is more to show that we are *good*, or that "we are true by *being* true."[48]

This has been a short summary of McLaren's thought. Yet he is just one of the leaders of the Emerging Church. Let us now turn to look at the main lines of thought in the work of Tony Jones.

TONY JONES

The Present Mind-set

Right from the start, in his *Postmodern Youth Ministry,* Tony Jones reminds youth workers that we are living in a time in which many of our presuppositions of how to do ministry (especially youth ministry) are being called into question. As we have seen in our surveys of Grenz, Franke, Hauerwas, Kallenberg, and McLaren, Jones tells us that the cul-

---

[46] E.g., ibid., 149.
[47] E.g., McLaren, *More Ready Than You Realize,* 134ff.
[48] Ibid., 61. The quote is from e-mail correspondence with Jones, June 22, 2004.

ture has changed, so that if we are "playing" by the rules of the Enlightenment, or modernity, we are using an outdated rulebook.[49] As Jones puts it, "more and more of our students are seeing the world with postmodern eyes,"[50] so we need to understand postmoderns and how we can communicate with them.

What are some of these key changes? In a very helpful section, Jones spends considerable time and space comparing the values of those who live with a modern mind-set (e.g., "Boomers") and those with a postmodern one. "Gen-Xers" came of age during the transition between modern and postmodern thought, but in Jones's view, "Millennials" are being taught "full-blown, no-holds-barred postmodern thought."[51] Here are descriptions of some of the values Jones compares:[52]

Modern Values	Postmodern Values
Rational: A key Enlightenment emphasis was on the adequacy of human reason to comprehend universal truths, and this primarily is achieved through science and the scientific method.	*Experiential:* Postmoderns want to experience things rather than just read or hear about them. For example, they want to experience interactive video games, or high-adventure vacations.
Scientific: So strong has been the belief in the superiority of science to any other discipline that scientism (the belief that only what science tells us is true and reasonable, is in fact true and reasonable) has become deeply embedded in our cultural mind-set.[53] Scientists have been the high priests of this worldview. Even God can and should be studied scientifically.	*Spiritual:* While popular interest in spiritual things waned under the influence of modern science, today spirituality is in! And people are willing to use innovative means to try to be spiritual.
Unanimity: Communities tended to be homogeneous, not multicultural. Religious options were few, even for dating (certainly not Catholics with Protestants).	*Pluralistic:* Spirituality takes on many forms, some of which have nothing to do with believing in God. Others will want to know who or what you mean by "God." As Jones wisely observes, technology has made

---

[49] Jones, *Postmodern Youth Ministry*, 23.
[50] Ibid., 12.
[51] Ibid., 29.
[52] For his comparisons, see ibid., 30-37.
[53] This has been the case, says Jones, even though scientism is self-refuting (it is not a statement of science).

	"everything available to everyone," and religiously the "choices are overwhelming."[54]
Exclusive: Most Americans agreed with the Judeo-Christian worldview, at least in terms of morality.	*Relative:* The emphasis on pluralism leads people to think that "all faiths contain elements of truth and any religion is a perfectly good way to express your spirituality."[55]
Egocentric: Modern philosophers stressed the importance of the self. In ethics, that stress focused on the autonomy of the self. Culturally, this view gave birth to the name the "Me" generation for the Boomers, with an emphasis on self-fulfillment.	*Altruistic:* Here, Jones notes an important paradox: Millennials seem to be even more "consumeristic" than their parents, yet they also highly value giving away their time and resources.
Individualistic: With the heavy emphasis on self-fulfillment, modern marketing efforts targeted the individual consumer.	*Communal:* In response to the emphasis on the self, postmoderns are returning to the family and community, but in "untraditional ways such as cohousing."[56] TV shows such as "Survivor," "Big Brother," and "Friends" capitalize on this interest.
Functional: The stress in modern architecture and technology has been on usefulness to serve a purpose. For instance, the "worship center" replaced the "sanctuary."	*Creative:* Here Jones observes that "Gen-Xers and Yers are known for their aesthetic sensibilities."[57] Beauty for its own sake is highly valued.
Industrial: The goals of the industrial age were "efficiency and material bounty,"[58] and machines were highly valued for their ability to contribute to these goals.	*Environmental:* In response to exploitation of the Earth's resources, students are concerned about the environment and its longer-term viability.
Local: People's interests were largely local, despite transportation improvements. Youth group overseas missionary trips were "virtually	*Global:* Jones puts it best when he writes: "With no major wars or economic depressions to unite us, students believe they're citizens of the

---

54 Jones, ibid., 31.
55 Ibid., 33.
56 Ibid., 35.
57 Ibid.
58 Ibid., 34.

unheard of,"[59] and communication with missionaries took place via "snail mail."

world, and their loyalties may be stronger to the entire human race than they are to nations. CNN and the Internet only strengthen this conviction."[60]

Compartmentalized: One's life and character at work could be separated from life on Sundays at church. We could live segmented lives. People did not practice what they preached in all areas of life.

Holistic: Integrity in *all* aspects of life is very important. Postmoderns are *rightly* suspicious of those who live segmented, compartmentalized lives.

Relevant: Make the gospel relevant to people's daily lives. Be seeker-sensitive.

Authentic: Be real. Be full of integrity in all areas of life. Jones puts it well: "Today, the younger generations respond [to appeals to relevance of the Bible to our daily lives], 'Don't tell me how to apply this Bible passage to my life. You don't know anything about my life. Just tell me what it really means. I'll decide how to apply it.'"[61]

For Jones, the question then arises, How then do we engage people with a postmodern mind-set? Obviously, from this list, using modern values and their related approaches will not impress these people. So, Jones rightly points out that youth ministers will have to become careful students of the broader culture in order to engage it.[62] We need to live as Christian missionaries in a foreign culture, since American culture is post-Christian.[63] Like missionaries abroad, we have to learn the "language" of the broader culture.

What specific cultural traits must youth ministers take into account? One is the rise of mysticism and spirituality. As Jones puts it, "propositional truth is out and mysticism is in. People are not necessarily put off by a religion that does not 'make sense'—they are more concerned with whether a religion can bring them into contact with God."[64] Another

[59] Ibid., 36.
[60] Ibid., 37.
[61] Ibid.
[62] Ibid., 46.
[63] Ibid., 47.
[64] Ibid., 63.

cultural trait is religious pluralism, which "embraces everyone except those who claim exclusivity."[65] That is, while it is politically correct to be accepting of many forms of spirituality, that kind of tolerance does not extend to those who claim their way is the unique and sole way to God.

According to Jones, another key aspect to understanding the postmodern ethos is *deconstructionism*. Jones defines deconstructionism as "a philosophical movement and theory of literary criticism that questions traditional assumptions about certainty, identity, and truth, and asserts that words can only refer to other words, and attempts to demonstrate how statements about any text subvert their own meanings."[66] As we saw above in McLaren's views, the heart of deconstructionism is the idea that you cannot get at and know the intention of an author when he or she wrote a text, and there is no fixed meaning in any text. That is because there are no identities; meanings, like anything else, always change, and are subject to what each reader brings to the text. Deconstructionism causes people to question everything, and when we do, we often find that behind the scenes, what really is motivating some viewpoint is a quest for power. Yet, according to Jones, this is not something to be feared; rather, "the beauty of the Spirit controlling the text is that it can, indeed, have different meanings in different times . . . and that the Spirit can use our own experiences and viewpoints to enlighten us to the meaning of the Word."[67]

In Jones's opinion, in a postmodern world there is no objective, universal truth. Instead, all is relative.[68] Here we see a difference of opinion between Jones and others, like Hauerwas, whom we read about before. Hauerwas does not think we are left in a position of relativism. Yet, from his experience as a youth pastor, Jones writes that postmodernism leaves us in a relativistic situation, and that our students are facing that every day. For them, "perception is reality."[69] But for Jones, as for Hauerwas, this situation is not a hindrance to the spread of the gospel, for we still can show the truthfulness of the gospel story by how we live out the

---

[65] Ibid., 67.
[66] Ibid., 20.
[67] Jones, private e-mail correspondence on June 22, 2004.
[68] Jones, *Postmodern Youth Ministry,* 26.
[69] Ibid., 28.

Christian life in community. This is like the emphasis we have seen placed on "embodied apologetics" by Hauerwas, Kallenberg, Grenz, Franke, and McLaren. This is why Jones claims that the most important priority for Christians is building a living, breathing community of believers that embodies and truly lives out the faith, so that outsiders can see the truthfulness of our story.[70]

What can outsiders find in such a community? We already have seen some values that help believers live out their faith in ways that communicate powerfully with postmoderns, such as authenticity and integrity, and living life holistically, so that our faith permeates all aspects of our lives. This is a good emphasis of postmodernism that should be embraced by Christians, for clearly Jesus is to be Lord over all areas of life, and not just on Sundays at church. We should live out our lives as sold-out disciples of Jesus. As part of that witness, Christians need to have healthy families and strong friendships, and we need to practice the spiritual disciplines, so as to have a witness beyond just words.

How should worship look to postmoderns? For Jones, worship needs to engage *all* the senses, in our architecture and lighting, in word, in music, in posture (e.g., kneeling), and even in smell (e.g., incense). Why does this matter? Jones explains that the Roman Catholic Church, as well as high Episcopalian and Eastern Orthodox churches, are attractive to younger generations because "they offer *transcendence* in worship."[71] How might this be the case? Such churches appeal to postmoderns' value for art and experience of God, who must dwell in a different kind of "place" than we do. Thus, it should look different than what we experience on a daily basis. Postmoderns want to be tied to tradition and to the past, so they want to know and understand the meaning of the symbols used in worship.[72]

Discipleship also would look different in a postmodern approach. Like worship and evangelism, discipleship should be done in community, and not in isolation, for it is in this context that new believers get to see how the life of Jesus should be lived out. Youth ministers need to provide situations that help their students experience the reality of the faith. For instance, we can help bring the Bible to life by emphasizing its

---

[70] Ibid., 82.
[71] Ibid., 97 (emphasis mine).
[72] Ibid., 164.

stories and their contexts, and we can help students put themselves into the stories.

It is the building up of the Christian community that Jones thinks will witness to postmoderns, and he is quite optimistic about the prospects for reaching them with the gospel. How should believers live out their faith in postmodern times to help share the story of Jesus in ways that postmoderns will be able to hear and understand? Here Jones offers several practical suggestions, as well as the more theoretical considerations that are driving his view as to why Christians ought to "postmodernize" the faith. Some of these latter ideas will be familiar, seen already in the views of Grenz, Franke, Hauerwas, Kallenberg, and McLaren. But he offers some additional specifics, and these will give us some insights into what Nancey Murphy, one of his mentors at Fuller, teaches.

Jones believes that by buying too much into modern emphases on the superiority of human reason, we have tended to treat evangelism as getting people to just *believe, or accept, the proposition* that Jesus is the only way to God, and that He is the only provision for our sin. So, Jones thinks that according to a modern view, "if an individual intellectually assents to John 3:16 or some other propositional statement of the gospel, then that person has been won."[73] But as we all know, mere intellectual assent does not mean that people actually *trust* in Christ to save them from their sins. So Jones is right when he points out that evangelism is not just a cognitive, intellectual process. After all, the demons believe God is real, and they tremble (James 2:19). They believe the fact that God exists, but they do not trust in Him. If people merely intellectually assent to the claims of Christ, it does not mean they then will change their lives in any significant way and become His disciples. This leads Jones to assert that "we must end the false dichotomy between justification and sanctification."[74] As we have seen in our other authors, Jones thinks *"salvation is a complex process that involves the individual and the community and results in a disciple who bears fruit."*[75] Justification (historically understood by Protestants to be the judicial act

---

[73] Ibid., 128.
[74] Ibid., 133.
[75] Ibid., 119 (emphasis in original).

by which God declares us righteous by faith in Jesus' death and resurrection, to save us from our sins) is blurred with sanctification (the process of becoming Christlike).

Instead of emphasizing biblical truths presented as propositions to be rationally accepted (a trait of the modern approach, he claims), we need to invite students and others into our Christian communities, in which they will see believers living out the faith authentically. That is, people need to be able to come into our communities and see Jesus living in us. Jones puts it well: "He [Jesus] offers life. He offers a transforming and accepting community of faith. He offers truth—truth that comes to life in community."[76]

Jones's emphasis on our need to embody and live out the gospel message is right on target. We should be people of integrity, who love Jesus with all our hearts, souls, minds, and strength, and we should love our neighbors as ourselves (Matt. 22:37; Mark 12:30; Deut. 6:5). After all, Jesus Himself says that all people will know that we are His disciples by our love for one another (John 13:35).

But there is a further motivation for Jones's emphasis, one that is derived from postmodern philosophy and not strictly from Scripture. We have seen similar points already raised by Grenz, Franke, Hauerwas, and Kallenberg, and touched on by McLaren, so here I will focus on the main epistemological ideas that are helping to drive Jones's practical theology. Here too we will see why he thinks believers should "postmodernize" the faith, or see it through postmodern glasses. We will also get a glimpse of some of the views Jones has learned from Nancey Murphy, a leading spokesperson for how Christianity ought to be conceived along postmodern lines.[77]

The Problem with Foundationalism, and the Holistic Solution

Like Murphy, Jones has come to think that Enlightenment-based epistemology is irremediably flawed and dead and needs to be discarded. According to him, foundationalism is the view that we can "base" or

---

[76] Ibid., 129.
[77] For example, see her *Beyond Liberalism and Fundamentalism: How Modern and Postmodern Philosophy Set the Theological Agenda*, Rockwell Lecture Series (Harrisburg, Pa.: Trinity Press International, 1996).

"ground" our beliefs upon a set of "foundational" beliefs that allow us to know how things *really* are—i.e., objectively. Just like Murphy, as well as Grenz, Franke, and McLaren, Jones asserts that foundationalism is the view that the foundational beliefs give us *certain, indubitable* knowledge, such that we *cannot* be mistaken about them.[78]

Earlier, I mentioned that requiring certainty for knowledge is too high a standard. Now, Jones agrees with me on this philosophically. However, as he puts it, "the problem is not with what philosophers believe, but with the way pastors act. . . . [M]any EV ["evangelical," I assume] pastors speak, preach, and write with a tone of such certainty that it is ultimately offputting to many 'seekers.'"[79] So here we see that the issue with foundationalism in part is not so much a philosophical one but rather the behaviors and attitudes that stem from it, that in turn impact how we reach out to certain kinds of people today.

Jones further claims that postmodern philosophers, such as Murphy, have shown that all our conclusions are based on our own subjective interpretations. We cannot get away from our own interpretive "grids," or our "glasses," if you will, and particular foundationalists would tend to choose their own preferred foundations, which would lead them where they wanted to go anyway.[80] We bring our subjective biases and experiences to bear when we read Scripture (or any other text, for that matter). All of our contexts (e.g., cultural, familial) influence and shape us.

What is the result of this? We *cannot* be objective, Jones claims.[81] For him, there simply is no neutral place to stand and interpret anything—any event, any text, etc. We are subjects trapped in human skin, and we necessarily have subjective viewpoints. We cannot get "past" our backgrounds, our perspectives, and our historically situated, conditioned experiences. Experience affects doctrine, and doctrine affects experience. We cannot get outside of our experiences and subjectively conditioned viewpoint to know truth with a capital "T," if you will. That is, we *cannot* know how things really are, in an objective sense.

---

[78] For Jones, see *Postmodern Youth Ministry*, 18. For Murphy, see *Beyond Liberalism*, 12-13. For Grenz and Franke, see *Beyond Foundationalism: Shaping Theology in a Postmodern Context* (Louisville: Westminster/John Knox, 2001), 30.

[79] Jones, private e-mail correspondence, June 22, 2004.

[80] Ibid.

[81] E.g., see Jones, *Postmodern Youth Ministry*, 74 ("no one . . . objectively approaches a text").

This is the main, underlying reason why postmodernists reject foundationalism, for foundationalism works hand-in-hand with the view that we can know reality as it is in itself.

So, what exactly is preventing us from knowing reality objectively? Once again, it is language. In perhaps his clearest statement of his view, Jones tells us that the "content of a belief system is inseparable from and dependent upon its language."[82] It is the same idea we have seen before: language and world are internally related. Further, Jones fleshes out the same idea we have seen in the four authors we looked at in chapter 2, that it is Christian language (our words, concepts, symbols, traditions, doctrines, and values) that sets us apart from other people.[83] Murphy concurs: "The biblical narratives *create* a world, and it is within this world that believers are to live their lives and understand reality."[84]

There are implications of Jones's view for apologetics. No longer do we need to "prove" (i.e., using human reason, and with certainty) the truth of the faith. For instance, we do not need to engage in rationalistic apologetics that tries to defend the objective truth of the resurrection as a historical fact. Why? Jones is quite clear: "It has only been since the Enlightenment that historians and reporters have propagated the lie that they are composing the true, factual, neutral, and objective account of an event or a person."[85] We all have our biases and particular, subjective viewpoints. For Jones, those who believe already that the Bible is God's Word cannot be objective about it, precisely because we believe that, and because we love it.[86]

As in the case of McLaren, I think Jones mixes and closely weds together the notions of objectivity and neutrality. He seems to think that Enlightenment-based thinkers believe that you have to be neutral (i.e., disinterested) in order to be objective. But (he seems to respond) since all of us bring our beliefs, presuppositions, cultural backgrounds, experiences, etc., to any text or experience, we simply cannot discard them and be neutral and disinterested about our claims. We cannot get

---

[82] Ibid., 151.
[83] Ibid., 146.
[84] Murphy, *Anglo-American Postmodernity*, 120 (emphasis mine).
[85] Jones, *Postmodern Youth Ministry*, 203.
[86] Ibid., 204; also from e-mail correspondence, June 22, 2004.

beyond them, so we cannot know the objective facts of the matter. Here we may learn from Alasdair MacIntyre, whom Jones cites approvingly.[87] MacIntyre asserts that "facts . . . were a seventeenth-century invention."[88] That is, they are an Enlightenment fiction, based on the mistaken notion that we can know objective truth. So it should not surprise us when Jones asserts strongly that we should "stop looking for some objective Truth that is available when we delve into the text of the Bible."[89] Again, "in a world in which absolute, foundational truth is being overthrown in fields like mathematics, physics, philosophy, and language theory, it seems ludicrous that Christians would insist that ours is the one indubitably sure thing in the world."[90] Hence, it misses the point to stress that the Bible is inerrant, in light of both the way postmoderns tend to see things and Jones's reasons why believers ought to reconceive Christianity along postmodern lines.

Does this mean that the truth of our faith does not matter to Jones? Jones explains:

> Jesus says, "I am the way, and the truth, and the life. No one comes to the Father except through me." That is truth. But what that means to a student who's struggling to overcome a drug addiction—how Jesus is "the truth"—will necessarily be different than what it means to the student who's the captain of the basketball team and seems to have it all together. Jesus is the truth for both students, but he looks very different to each.[91]

Truth is not to be found from some supposed, nonexistent, neutral standpoint, says Jones. It comes only when we immerse ourselves within a community that has been formed by its language, and Christians claim

---

[87] Ibid., 214ff.

[88] Alasdair MacIntyre, *Whose Justice? Which Rationality?* (Notre Dame, Ind.: University of Notre Dame Press, 1988), 357.

[89] Jones, *Postmodern Youth Ministry*, 201.

[90] Ibid., 142. Here, I should observe that, contrary to his assertion in the book, foundationalism is alive and well in philosophy. See Michael DePaul's observation in *Resurrecting Old-Fashioned Foundationalism,* ed. Michael R. DePaul (Lanham, Md.: Rowman & Littlefield, 2001). DePaul, who is a philosopher, remarks that "foundationalism is alive and well; indeed, at least within Anglo-American analytic philosophy, I think it is safe to say that it remains the dominant position" (ibid., vii). In our e-mail correspondence, Jones realizes he overstated the case when he asserted that foundationalism is dead in philosophy.

[91] Jones, *Postmodern Youth Ministry*, 142.

that they uniquely have the truth. But again, even that truth is known only "from within" the standpoint, and the language, of the Christian community.

THE NEXT STEP

Now that we have completed our survey of what Christian postmoderns, and specifically what two key leaders of the Emerging Church, are claiming, we will turn to examine how postmodernism is at work in universities, both secular and Christian. After that survey, we will shift to assess Christian postmodernism's strengths and weaknesses.

"The basic contentions of the argument of this book are implicit in its title and subtitle, namely, that reality is socially constructed and that the sociology of knowledge must analyze the processes in which this occurs."

PETER L. BERGER AND THOMAS LUCKMANN
THE SOCIAL CONSTRUCTION OF REALITY:
A TREATISE IN THE SOCIOLOGY OF KNOWLEDGE, 1

"The key issues raised by the social constructivists [are] whether or not our public bodies of knowledge— especially the sciences—are about something, and whether or not they are only the handiwork of socio-political forces and biases; social constructivists want to challenge the view that external nature plays a decisive role in shaping what we know about it, that nature somehow 'leaks in' . . . and acts as a constraint in our knowledge constructing activities."

D. C. PHILLIPS
"HOW, WHY, WHAT, WHEN, AND WHERE:
PERSPECTIVES ON CONSTRUCTIVISM IN
PSYCHOLOGY AND EDUCATION," 5

FOUR

POSTMODERNISM GOES TO SCHOOL: THE STATE OF OUR UNIVERSITIES

Now that we have delineated the main ideas of postmodernism, both Christian and non-Christian, we should see how these ideas are influencing other areas of life. Here I will look at academic life. The effects of postmodernism are widespread, although the extent of its influence varies among Christian colleges and churches. We already have studied some of its influences in youth ministry. We will look at various disciplines within the universities, and we will examine the way postmodernism is affecting Christian and secular universities.

Before moving on, we should recall that, as concerns the influence of postmodernism, the secular universities are divided largely between the natural sciences and the humanities. Those working in the sciences still tend to believe that science gives us the truth about the world; this continues to be a deeply ingrained belief in our culture. But the humanities, with perhaps the exception of philosophy on the whole, basically have bought into postmodern thought.

One other brief, preliminary observation is in order. From my own experience, which is supported by the Barna poll we noted earlier, many Christian high school graduates are quite unprepared for the ideologies at work in at least the secular universities and even many Christian schools. Many come into college already assuming that ethics are relative to individuals or cultures, but even those who don't accept that assumption will face an onslaught of ideas in a wide range of classes that will challenge their Christian beliefs. The results could be several. For one, their faith and morals could be marginalized, relegated as it were to an "upper story," as Francis Schaeffer put it. They will be taught that to believe in Christianity is to take a leap of faith, to try to give life meaning, but that we really know life is objectively absurd (applying Darwinism consistently). That is, religious belief is not a matter of knowledge. Or, two, they might come out of college having rejected their faith. Or, three, they might still hold on to their faith but conclude that they have no reasons for it besides just taking the Scriptures on blind faith. Or, last, they might come out stronger, having had their faith challenged and tested, because they pressed on to find answers to critics' objections as well as reasons why we should believe in Christianity.

Now we are in a position to begin to examine the state of various academic disciplines, and we will start with secular colleges and universities before moving on to Christian ones.

THE SECULAR UNIVERSITIES TODAY

The Natural Sciences

Let us start with the hard sciences, such as chemistry and physics as well as biology. For the most part, the dominant view in secular schools is that Darwinism is right, despite its flaws, and that it is not only the most promising research paradigm but it also is the objective truth. Therefore, scientists will resist claims made by intelligent design (ID) theorists, such as Michael Behe or William Dembski, that ID also is a valid research paradigm, and a better one than Darwinism. Many will hold to these attitudes steadfastly due to their commitment to metaphysical naturalism, the worldview that there is no supernatural (or immaterial) aspect to the universe and that it can be fully explained by natural phenomena. Naturalism is still the reigning dogma in the natural sciences, at least in secular schools, and for scientists employed at such schools to publish articles advocating ID in their fields' journals is to commit academic suicide.

Some philosophers of science, however, have realized that Darwinism is a research paradigm and not dogma, and that a paradigm that better explains the phenomena in the world could supplant Darwinism. These people could be open, at least in principle, to considering ID or other paradigms. However, several such thinkers hold to an "anti-realist" view, which means that they do not think that science actually gives us the facts about the world. Instead, they believe, we work and do research within paradigms, and when paradigm (in our case, Darwinism) continues to run into difficulties it just cannot explain, then these philosophers would say that that would be the time to abandon it in favor of a new one. Even so, most Darwinists think that science gives us the facts about the world, and so they can be called "realists."

Much is at stake for any Darwinist who abandons Darwinism, or who even suggests that it could be wrong. Research grants, publication, promotion, and tenure all could be withheld or denied. Students too face ostracism or ridicule for anti-evolutionary views.

Though the reigning view in the hard sciences treats Darwinism in a realist way, as giving us the actual truth of the matter, there are post-modern paradigms in philosophy of science for how scientific work should be done.[1] If these paradigms make much further inroads, the natural sciences themselves could face great pressure to give up a realist approach. For example, if naturalism can be shown to be just a human construction and not the objective truth (which I think can be done), then the stage could be set for postmodern views of science to supplant the current dominant, realist interpretation of Darwinism.

Business

In business departments, many still approach their discipline as a science, and to that extent they will tend to resist postmodernism, for the same kinds of reasons the natural sciences do. But people are suspicious of business leaders and their motives, and this attitude is not without merit. Corporations may lay off large numbers of employees, claiming it is for the good of their profitability, yet shortly thereafter vote a huge bonus for the CEO. Corporate executives in the electricity industry may have asserted that they had no role to play in enormous rate increases in California, yet later we find out that internal documents corroborate our suspicions.

Large-scale scandals, such as those involving Enron and WorldCom, further support our suspicions. When these scandals occurred, many started to ask how we could trust the profitability statements of other cor-

---

[1] For instance, see Nancey Murphy, *Theology in the Age of Scientific Reasoning* (Ithaca, N.Y.: Cornell University Press, 1990).

porations, if they did not adhere to a common ethical standard. But truth may not be what matters. Richard Rorty suggests that truth may be a matter of what our peers let us get away with "saying."[2] And so we can have accounting reports that embellish, distort, or even misrepresent the truth.

If postmodernism takes a firm hold in business and law, then contracts could become unenforceable, except by a raw imposition of judicial power. People could say they agree and thus sign a contract, but later decide to break it. How would the dispute be resolved, if the meaning of the signers of the contract were not something others could know? After all, according to postmodern thought, we cannot know the authors' intent, so the meaning of a document is "up to us." If meaning is just a matter of how words are used within particular communities, how will we decide which are the relevant interpretive communities to decide the dispute? We are members of many "communities," and a person could claim membership in whichever community best suits his or her personal aims.

Furthermore, businesses often deal with rights of employees and other stakeholders, such as customers. But on postmodern views, rights are a fiction. They do not exist as universally true for all people, or even if they do, we cannot know them as such. Instead, rights are just constructions made by how we talk, and not objective, transcendent truths. There are no inalienable rights, on this view, so in principle there is no standard to protect people. Hence, why should we treat equals equally by giving them equal pay for their work? It cannot be based on some universal, ahistorical standard of justice, but instead it becomes a matter of the values of particular communities. Or, it becomes nothing but the raw imposition of power by a governmental body that has no moral basis for its decision.

Law

In law, contracts are but one area under assault. More and more, law is seen as a human product and not as something that transcends us. In postmodern thought, people are at least suspicious of claims that we know what are objectively true laws for all people. At worst, they out-

---

[2] Richard Rorty, *Philosophy and the Mirror of Nature* (Princeton, N.J.: Princeton University Press, 1979), 176.

right deny that we can know them. So our inalienable rights enumerated in the Constitution are but the product of a bygone way of talking, namely, that of liberalism. According to that view, based in Enlightenment thought, people thought they could know universal truths by their reason. But in postmodern thought, we realize that these are just human constructions, and they can be changed or deleted simply by changing how we talk, or, more directly, by judicial decree. Many judges now adjudicate not on the basis of natural law theory (universal, objective rights) but on the basis of mere personal opinion.

Oliver Wendell Holmes, Jr., who served on the U.S. Supreme Court from 1902 to 1932, helped to champion this view against universal natural law. As Michael S. Moore explains, for Holmes, the warrant for judicial review was only his feelings, "but since no one else's (no matter how numerous) are any better, I'll impose mine and not theirs."[3] Holmes urged that in morality and law we consider Darwin's teaching "and recognize that so long as nature preserves man's instinct to survive and prosper, it has endorsed the self-preferring impulse."[4]

In our postmodern times, law schools tend to teach that, since we cannot know the meaning of the framers of the Constitution (or of any other law), or that such intent is basically irrelevant, we must interpret the Constitution and find out *what it means to us now.* This belief finds its expression in the phrase "the living Constitution," for it is not a static document but one that continually must be constructed and reconstructed according to how we talk and live today. Postmodern thought also would have us believe that those in power do not make laws on the basis of universal moral standards but instead on the basis of either (1) their own will to power or (2) a desire to provide procedural fairness. Justice in a democracy can become just a matter of making the game fair for everyone, without any overarching standard as to what justice is or why it is so valuable. As Alasdair MacIntyre asserts, there is no such thing as justice as such; there are only the "justices" of many different groups of people.[5]

---

[3] Michael S. Moore, "Law as a Functional Kind," in *Natural Law Theory,* ed. Robert P. George (Oxford: Clarendon, 1994), 230.
[4] Mark DeWolfe Howe, "Introduction," in Oliver Wendell Holmes, *The Common Law,* ed. Mark DeWolfe Howe (Boston: Little, Brown, 1963), xxvi.
[5] See his *Whose Justice? Which Rationality?* (Notre Dame, Ind.: University of Notre Dame Press, 1988). MacIntyre has had a very significant influence on Hauerwas, Kallenberg, Murphy, and Jones.

Religious Studies

As you might imagine, religion in the secular schools is highly influenced by postmodern thought. It seems axiomatic within secular academia that religion does not give us objective truth but only the constructions of individuals or social groups. This is the legacy of Kant and those who have followed him.

In secular universities, there is an emphasis on studying religion from a variety of perspectives, such as feminist, African-American, womanist, Hindu, Muslim, and many others. Here, the implicit (and sometimes explicit) message is that no one has the corner on the market of religious truth; in fact, no one has knowledge of objective truth. Instead, there are just many truths, and thus we all should be tolerant of each other. Furthermore, postmodernism makes us mindful of marginalized, "oppressed voices," and so religion scholars may give extra credence to so-called "secret Gospels," even though they were not recognized as authoritative by the early church. Evangelical Christian groups can encounter much opposition from university administrators if they are seen as advocating exclusivity. For instance, if they require their members to be only born-again Christians, that student group might be kicked off campus.

Furthermore, religion might be studied from other standpoints, such as sociology (which can be quite interesting and insightful), ethics, or history. But usually it is not studied from the standpoint of trying to find out which is the true religion. After all, if religion is just up to us, who are we to impose our beliefs on someone else? Even so, there are professors who have their own agendas and axes to grind, who will advocate, say, atheism as a direct challenge to Christians.

Sociology

I have studied sociology of religion, so I will confine my remarks on sociology to that subfield. Sociologists do ethnographic field research with a view to describing their subjects accurately and then offering a broader explanation and application of their findings. For instance, this is the kind of project undertaken by Robert Bellah and his coauthors in *Habits of the Heart*. Sociologists vary, however, in their philosophical assumptions about our abilities to know objective reality. As an example, Freud was very influenced by scientism, the view that only what science can know is true and reasonable is in fact true and reasonable. He also accepted empiricism, so he believed that anything that cannot be known by the five senses is not an item of knowledge. Consequently, he believed that religious views are not scientific, and religious claims to know objective truth are mistaken. Clearly, sociologists following Freud's views would dismiss religious claims to know objective truth as mere projections, or constructions of our obsessive neuroses. Marx, too, thought religion to be just a functional device to keep the proletariat pacified and under the control of the bourgeoisie. Religion certainly could not give us objective truth about a deity.

On the other hand, there have been other sociologists who have held in varying ways that religion can give us contact with an irreducibly religious reality. William James thought that religion is mainly a matter of individuals' feelings and awarenesses of what they take to be the divine. So experience of actual, irreducibly religious phenomena is possible. Mircea Eliade thought that religion is something irreducible, and the sacred can be experienced in different ways. He believed we could have direct awareness of the sacred, which might be understood differently in various cultural settings.

There has been one particular sociologist, however, whose work has influenced at least Stanley Grenz and John Franke among the authors we are examining in this text, and that is Peter Berger. Grenz and Franke refer to Berger's claim that human reality is socially constructed in support of their own claim that "we do not inhabit the 'world-in-itself'; instead, we live in a linguistic world of our own making."[6] What does Berger mean by the "social construction of reality"?[7] Berger draws upon a Kantian kind of distinction between a realm of facts known by science through empirical observation and a realm that is private and subjective. His sociological method for religious study stresses observable behavior while bracketing one's own philosophical and theological presuppositions. The function of religion, he claims, is to erect a "sacred canopy" that gives meaning to the social order and life therein. We erect

---

[6] Stanley Grenz and John Franke, *Beyond Foundationalism: Shaping Theology in a Postmodern Context* (Louisville: Westminster/John Knox, 2001), 53.
[7] See Peter L. Berger and Thomas Luckmann, *The Social Construction of Reality* (New York: Anchor Books/Doubleday, 1966).

the canopy by externalizing, or pouring out, our spirits into the world and universe. Then, we tend to forget that these views are just human constructs, and we tend to "objectivate" them. Last, we tend to internalize them, so that these "realities" shape our very way of thinking. It is possible, on Berger's view, that a particular canopy's view of ultimate reality could match up with objective reality, but as sociologists we must consider just the human aspects of its construction.

A philosopher whose writings have influenced both sociologists and Christian postmodernists is Alasdair MacIntyre. MacIntyre thinks that all rationality is dependent on particular traditions, for there is no rationality-as-such.[8] Nor are there facts; they were merely a seventeenth-century invention.[9] There are no self-evident truths[10] according to his view, either, for it seems that, according to his view, we always work within language.[11]

Thus, in sociology, it makes a key difference whether someone adopts a methodology informed by a thinker who believes we can know objective reality. For those influenced by the social constructionist views, I think that in some respects, sociology benefits from the postmodern emphasis on the particularity of people. This stress makes researchers study carefully the particular beliefs and context of a people. This emphasis also should make researchers cautious when making generalizations.

English

I worked closely with English graduate students who were fellow expository writing teachers during my doctoral studies. There I saw a set of attitudes that led me to think that English departments tend to be the ones *most* influenced by postmodernism.

First, there is an affinity between English as a discipline and postmodernism. This is due to the nature of the field. We have to read authors and interpret their works. So we carefully focus on authors and their meanings, the genres, and the authors' context, including the historical times in which they wrote. In English, we deliberately focus in

---

[8] Alasdair MacIntyre, *Whose Justice? Which Rationality?* 346.
[9] Ibid., 357.
[10] Alasdair MacIntyre, *After Virtue,* 2nd ed. (Notre Dame, Ind.: University of Notre Dame Press, 1984), 69.
[11] See my *Virtue Ethics and Moral Knowledge: Philosophy of Language After MacIntyre and Hauerwas* (Aldershot, England: Ashgate, 2003), chapter 2.

part on stories, or narratives, as a kind of genre, instead of, say, analytic arguments in philosophy. It also is a field that has felt acutely the influence of Derrida's deconstructionism.

Second, assignments are given in writing classes that encourage (or even require) the students to explicitly *construct their own identities.* What does this mean? Most fundamentally, one's identity, philosophically speaking, is one's essence, or soul. For example, I have a human soul, and it is my particular soul, and not someone else's. But there also is a *sense* of one's own identity—that is, how do I see myself? For instance, I will describe myself in different settings as a Christ-follower, husband, father, or ethics professor working in religion and philosophy. But this latter kind of identity presupposes the former, that I exist as a human being, and there is something about me that makes me *me* through time and change. That is my soul.

What should we make of a writing assignment that was given to undergraduates that asked them to write a paper that constructs their identity? The assignment, given at the University of Southern California, did not make a distinction between the two kinds of identities I mentioned above; instead, it seemed to leave it open-ended and up to the student. This left students with the idea that what they *are* is something that is entirely up to them. One key way this was worked out was to have students construct their gender. Teachers would assume that while sex is biologically given, nonetheless gender and gender roles are up to us. So, people were free to construct their gender as being gay, lesbian, bisexual, straight, etc.

History

For some time now students have faced a multiplicity of perspectives in the college-level study of history. The attitude has been that we cannot have simply a white, Anglo-Saxon, male interpretation of some events. Now we must have representatives from many "voices," or perspectives. Why must this be the case? Because, according to the postmodern view, there is no such thing as history as such; there are only *histories.* Why? Because we simply cannot know the objective facts that took place. As many cultures, communities, or people groups as exist in relation to some event (or set of events), there will be (in principle, at least) that many histories.

Now, we should be careful not to dismiss this viewpoint too quickly, for there are certain aspects to it that are true. For instance, postmodernists are right to point out that authors do have particular points of view, and as McLaren and Jones point out, they tend to focus on those aspects of interest to them. To give an example, it is very hard for a white author who has grown up in suburban America to enter into the experiences of African-American people from inner city New York who have suffered the overt and subtler effects of white racism. So, it is very helpful to gain others' perspectives on events and issues. But that does not mean that there isn't objective truth there to be found and told in history books. There are facts of the matter: for example, the World Trade Center towers were in fact destroyed on September 11, 2001 by terrorists who flew planes into them. Yes, there are many viewpoints on that event: those of fellow terrorists; Muslims who are American citizens; rescue workers; survivors of the attacks; and family and friends who lost loved ones in the attacks, to name but a few. But the existence of different perspectives on an event does not negate the fact that one single, objective event actually occurred. While there may be various interpretations of an event, that does not mean that *all* we may know are nothing but our interpretations.

Psychology

Similar to what we already have seen in English departments, psychology faces an issue as to how therapists should work with their patients. That is, if the self is as malleable as many seem to think it is, then therapists should not impose their own preferences or values on patients. Hence, for example, it would be immoral for a therapist to try to help a patient overcome habituated homosexual behavior unless the patient wants to change. After all, who is the therapist to say that what someone does is wrong? Yet there *are* various behavioral patterns that virtually everyone sees as wrong, including various ones that are labeled as dysfunctional. For example, therapists pretty much universally recognize codependency as a behavioral pattern that they should help a person overcome.

In general, however, while psychologists will speak of the "self," nonetheless they seem to have lost a clear idea of what the self is and what is appropriate for the person. This is a direct result of the loss of the understanding that we are embodied souls, created in God's image, and that the image of God in us fundamentally circumscribes what is and is not appropriate for us. To put it differently, we have lost a clear sense of what human nature is. (As an aside, I think this also keenly affects our culture's view of abortion, in that many see personhood as merely something that we construct.) We live in a day in which human nature has been dismissed as unscientific (who can empirically test that which is immaterial?). Now, due to postmodern influences, human nature is being treated as a human construct, and so quite simply we have lost a shared consensus as to what are the boundary conditions for good, appropriate human behavior. If anyone tries to speak out and tell us what is right, then the typical outcry will be, "Who are you to impose your beliefs on me?"

Education

Constructivism is alive and well in educational theory, and in some cases this has been quite helpful. *Psychological constructivism* has both moderate and extreme forms. In the former, theorists place emphasis on active learning and learner-centered education, which can be very helpful. Rather than focus on lecture-driven teaching techniques, active learning involves students in various participatory activities and roles, so they are not passive recipients of dispensed information. This moderate form of psychological constructivism does not entail that we somehow construct the world. The more extreme form, however, "denies access to an observer-independent reality."[12] According to this view, our "knowledge" cannot be of objective reality; knowledge is a human construction.

Another form of constructivism in education is *social constructionism,* and such theorists "are primarily concerned with how public bodies of knowledge are constructed."[13] D. C. Phillips points out that

---

[12] Peggy Velis, "An Overview of Constructivism in Education," unpublished paper, Biola University, 2003, 6. I am indebted to my colleague's understanding of constructionism in education.
[13] Ibid., 3.

the key issues raised by the social constructivists is whether or not our public bodies of knowledge—especially the sciences—are about something, and whether or not they are only the handiwork of socio-political forces and biases; social constructivists want to challenge the view that external nature plays a decisive role in shaping what we know about it, that nature somehow "leaks in" . . . and acts as a constraint in our knowledge constructing activities.[14]

Thus the more radical proponents of both psychological constructivism and social constructivism hold that we do not have cognitive access to the world as it really is, just as we saw in the postmodern authors we have been discussing. These psychological and social constructivists also hold that people build up their own bodies of knowledge not by discovering objective truths about the real world but by their construction of that knowledge and of that world.

These insights into constructivism in education have relevance also to mathematics. We would tend to think that mathematics, with its appeal to precise calculations and equations, and thus correct answers, would be immune to postmodern, constructivist thought. But that is not necessarily the case. Steve Woolgar, a social constructivist, observes that

It should be clear . . . that mathematical statements such as 2+2=4 are as much a legitimate target of sociological questioning as any other item of knowledge. . . . What kinds of historical conditions gave their expression currency and, in particular, what established (and now sustains) it as a belief? This kind of question is posed without regard for the (actual) truth status of the statement.[15]

So even mathematics is not immune from such constructivist approaches.

If the foregoing surveys are right about the state of secular universities, we would expect (or at least hope) that Christian schools would

[14] D. C. Phillips, "How, Why, What, When, and Where: Perspectives on Constructivism in Psychology and Education," *Issues in Education* 3:2 (1997): 5, accessed through Academic Search Premier, January 22, 2004.
[15] Steve Woolgar, *Science: The Very Idea* (New York: Routledge, 1993), 43, cited in Phillips, "How, Why, What, When, and Where." Again, I am indebted to Peggy Velis for her insights into the influence of constructivist thought in mathematics.

be resisting this movement. But that is not always the case, as we will now see.

CHRISTIAN COLLEGES AND UNIVERSITIES

While we might expect Christian college-level education to resist postmodern influences by holding to a robust view of truth and our ability to know it, this just may not be the case. Getting a doctoral degree from a university with any prestige at all usually requires that students go to secular (or secularized) schools. When Christians go on to pursue doctorates, they will encounter these postmodern influences, not to mention naturalistic ones, and they will have to come to some sort of resolution between these views and Christianity. In turn, they bring their viewpoints into Christian colleges as faculty.

Another problem is that there have been very few Christian programs that equip their students with reasons for their faith in ways more than knowing what the Bible says about various topics. This is due in large measure to our inheriting the fallout of the fundamentalist-liberal controversies in the early twentieth century, as a result of which fundamentalists tended to hold fast to the authority of the Bible but basically gave up on reason as a way to help us know the truth of Christianity. This anti-intellectual spirit still affects us today and is often manifested in the form of a suspicion toward academic truth claims in general and philosophy (which medieval scholars called the handmaid of theology) in particular.

Rejection of the Bible's authority is one of the first challenges Christians will experience in secular academia. If they have not been well grounded in how to support their faith against such challenges, they likely will need to find a way to reduce the tension between their received Christian faith and their academic discipline's presuppositions. That could take place by rejecting their faith, or key aspects of it, such as the inerrancy of Scripture or even its authority. Or, they could find ways to accommodate their Christian beliefs by modifying them in order to accept both their discipline's core ideas and key aspects of the faith.

On the other hand, some Christians are seeking out postmodernist mentors in various programs because they think that we do indeed need to postmodernize the faith. So when Christians graduate from doctoral programs, they may well emerge with the mind-set of their postmodernist teachers. This may mean that these graduates will reject traditional aspects of our historical understanding of the faith, such as our belief that we can know that Christian doctrines (e.g., the resurrection) are objectively true.

Put simply, the mere fact that a college claims to be Christian (even evangelical) is no guarantee that the traditional, orthodox understanding of the faith will be taught there. You have to understand the extent to which various ideas have impacted that particular school. There are certain key areas within which postmodernism is having significant effects. The first of these has to do with the inerrancy of Scripture. While traditional Christian schools will affirm the authority of Scripture, they may well have given up on inerrancy. This may be a response to higher criticism and its attacks against the accuracy of the Old and New Testaments. But, as we saw in the previous chapter, postmodernists have their own reasons for rejecting the notion of inerrancy as a fruitful way of *talking*. While they will affirm Scripture as the normative standard by which Christians should live, behave, and talk (hence calling the Bible the Christians' "grammar"), they have given up on the ability to determine if it is without error. Such ability, they would say, would presuppose an ability to compare the Scriptures with reality. But as we have seen already, they have given up on the ability to know objective reality. So, to talk about inerrancy is to continue to buy into a bygone way of talking and thinking, namely, an Enlightenment-modernist view that we can know the universal truth of a matter. On the other hand, by committing itself to inerrancy, a college will tend to resist postmodernism.

There are other areas of influence of postmodernism in Christian schools. Theology is a key one, for as we have seen, Hauerwas, Grenz, and Franke explicitly teach in theology, and Kallenberg teaches in philosophical theology. English is another, for reasons we explored above. Again, each college or seminary will have to be evaluated on its own. There is a growing trend among Christians to try to recast our understanding of the faith in a postmodern way, and the number of academic publications by postmodernist thinkers (such as much literature available on the Emerging Church) seems to be growing especially in the areas of theology, philosophy, ethics, and practical ministry.

CONCLUSION

These are examples of how postmodernism is at work in our universities, both secular and Christian. I have not tried to present a thorough analysis of exactly how, and to what extent, postmodernism is influencing each of these arenas. My intent has been to provide a sweeping overview of many ways it is shaping our academic institutions. My hope is that with these insights, readers may be able to discern just how postmodernism has helped shape a particular school.

The time has come to begin to evaluate postmodernism, especially as it affects Christians. To what extent should we accept it? Should we accept or reject it in total, or are there some things we should learn from it, while rejecting others? To these and other issues we now will turn in chapters 5, 6, and 7, before we press on to address relativism in chapter 8, and my positive case for securing knowledge of objective truth in chapter 9.

"Language does not represent reality,
it constitutes reality."

BRAD J. KALLENBERG
ETHICS AS GRAMMAR, 234

ANALYZING THE ROOTS OF POSTMODERNISM

Postmodern thought depends on several key beliefs, some typical ones of which are that (1) although a "real" world may exist, we cannot know it as such; and (2) the only way we can know anything about this "real" world is by our talking about it in the language of our community. But (3) we cannot know the essence of language, for that would be to know something as it really is. Instead, there are only languages-in-use in specific times and places. Thus, (4) our talking about reality shapes and "makes" it what it is for us—we "make" our world(s) by the use of our language(s) within our communities. Furthermore, (5) meanings are not some universal matter, either; they too are constructions made by the use of language within each community. Finally, (6) Christian postmodernists such as Hauerwas, Kallenberg, Grenz, and Franke agree that these points are true of the Christian community, or church, such that even though we say that Jesus is *the* truth, there still is no way within history to prove it as such.

What shall we make of these claims? In this chapter, I will examine two main issues by way of a more general critique of postmodernism. I first will analyze and critique its claim that we are on the "inside" of language and cannot get outside of it to know the real world. Second, I will look crucially at its claim that meaning is primarily a matter of behavior within a community, that it is not primarily a matter of the intentions of the individual person himself or herself. In chapter 6, we will examine issues with McLaren and Jones's views, and then in chapter 7 we will look at specific problems that surface for Christians and Christianity under this approach, especially in terms of theology, ethics, and ministry. In chapter 8, I will examine whether or not the views of

Christian postmodernists are relativistic, especially in light of their attempts to ward off that charge. And even if their views are relativistic, is that a problem?[1] Last, in chapter 9, I will explore how we can actually know objective truth.

THE ISSUE OF ACCESS

Let us begin with the view of Hauerwas, Kallenberg, Grenz, and Franke that we are on the "inside" of language and cannot get "outside" of it to know how things really (i.e., objectively) are.[2] In my opinion, this is the most important view to start with, since it is central to their whole view. If they are right, then only the details matter about what they say. We would have to change our way of seeing the world and agree that we simply cannot know reality. But if we find that they are mistaken, then much of their view will be compromised.

If they are right about this claim, then we would expect that truths are truly local in character and applicable only to particular communities. That is, what is true for one community may not be so for another. Despite this expectation, Hauerwas, Kallenberg, Grenz, and Franke all make broad, sweeping, seemingly universal assertions. By way of reminder, let us review many of these claims. Hauerwas claims that the gospel is the true story, which sounds like a bold, sweeping claim about all of reality. He also tells us that to see rightly, we must have a vision, and that that way of seeing the world depends on being part of a community and knowing its language. He claims that there is no realm of facts out there waiting for us to see apart from how we describe them in language. We do not get to know the world by just going out and looking at it. To know the world requires learning the language of a particular people, which he contends is the Christian one. And he emphasizes the importance of our being a community that witnesses to the truth of the gospel by how we live, and not by giving arguments that supposedly get at the nature of reality.

Kallenberg echoes many of these same ideas; in particular we

---

[1] I won't address all the issues these views face. For instance, I have decided not to address issues with the "narrative unity" of the self. But in *Virtue Ethics and Moral Knowledge: Philosophy of Language After MacIntyre and Hauerwas* (Aldershot, England: Ashgate, 2003), I go into detail about their views' specific features and problems. In that book I argue and counterargue at length with their views.
[2] See also my understanding of this concept on 40-41.

focused on his claims that we are indeed on the "inside" of language and cannot "escape" from its influences to know objective reality. He also wants us to learn to see the world *rightly*, that is, from a certain standpoint, namely, from the standpoint of the Christian story. Indeed, one of the chief confusions he wants to clear up is the belief that we can know reality apart from language use. That idea is mistaken, says Kallenberg, and he has learned the truth: each linguistic community makes its own world by the use of its language. Furthermore, we cannot experience reality apart from our conceptual lenses. All experience must involve interpretation.

Grenz and Franke are quite similar, too, for they too think that foundationalism is in shambles, and that we need to move on to a new way of seeing the world. The way to go, they think, is that of a linguistic "constructionism" like what we have seen in Kallenberg and Hauerwas. Grenz and Franke assert that we live in a linguistic world that we ourselves make. We cannot escape this limitation of language and somehow know reality from some supposedly neutral standpoint. Despite that limitation on what we can know, they, like Hauerwas and Kallenberg, still claim that the gospel is the truth.

All these are fascinating claims, and these four writers seem to make them in such a way as to indicate that they have found *the* truth. That is, they seem to write in such a way as to suggest that they have found the way all of us *should* see things, and not just that they are describing how they happen to see things. It is this character of their claims that we should examine most carefully.

If they are right that we cannot know reality as it is (i.e., objectively), then we construct the world(s) in which we live. One of the most remarkable traits about their writings is their effort to take their view seriously and consistently. So, to be fair, we should apply their own standards to their own works. In that case, what should we make of these many sweeping, seemingly universal truth claims? There seem to be only two options: either these claims are (1) just expressions of how they (or their community's members) have made their own world by the use of their language, or (2) they are much more—that is, they are claims that they know the way things *really* are, in an objective sense. If the former interpretation is correct, then their many claims are just those uttered from within a particular, local community, one in which its members happen to talk in such a way that that is how they have made their world. But if so, then why should any of us outside that specific, local community care? If the latter interpretation is true, then they presuppose what they deny—that is, an access to objective reality itself—in order to deny it! Let us explore each option in some more detail, to see which is right.

Hauerwas, Kallenberg, Grenz, and Franke have gone to great lengths to defend their idea that there is no essence, or objective, universal quality, that we can know as it is apart from how we talk about it. They are quite consistent when they draw the conclusion that there cannot be an essence to language, even Christian language. Alasdair MacIntyre, another author who philosophically has had significant influence on at least Hauerwas, Kallenberg, Jones, and Murphy, captures this point well. According to him, there cannot be some language as such (e.g., Latin); there can only be Latin as it was written and spoken at a certain time and place (e.g., in the time of Cicero in Rome).[3] Following his lead, we should conclude that there is no essence to Christian language; there is only the Christian language that is written and spoken in discrete Christian communities at particular times and places. As we have seen, Grenz and Franke agree with this view when they claim that all theological reflection is local.

This conclusion seems quite consistent with Grenz and Franke's overall views, as it is with those of Hauerwas and Kallenberg. So what is the relevant community out of which they each write or speak? They tell us that they write as Christians, and that other Christians should see things as they do. But for them to say that they are writing simply as Christians is not enough to inform us of the specific communities out of which they write. Christianity is not some monolithic, homogeneous religion; for example, there are Catholics, Protestants, and Orthodox, to name but a few main branches. Within Protestantism, there are many denominations, among which are Baptists, Presbyterians, Methodists, Pentecostals, Evangelical Free, and many more. Even this level of specificity is not enough. Take Baptists as one example; there are Conservative, American, and Southern Baptists, to name but three. Among Southern Baptists, there are different groupings too. For

---

[3] See his *Whose Justice? Which Rationality?* (Notre Dame, Ind.: University of Notre Dame Press, 1988), 357.

instance, there are more doctrinally conservative as opposed to more liberal people in the denomination. There also are Southern Baptist missionaries, who come from various parts of the world, who minister in other parts of the world. So which is the relevant community?

What we do not find in these authors is a clear statement as to the specific, local Christian communities out of which they write. Consider Kallenberg as an example. While never telling his readers which specific Christian community shapes his specific understanding, he nonetheless proceeds to tell us in quite general fashion how Christians ought to see the world. He does not tell us if his relevant Christian community was, for instance, Trinity Evangelical Free Church in Redlands, California, in 2001, or former students of Nancey Murphy at Fuller Theological Seminary in 1999, or some other particular community.

By not telling us what are the communities out of which Kallenberg, Hauerwas, Grenz, and Franke write, these writers can make seemingly sweeping, universal truth claims about how things are and how Christians ought to live. This seems to be a rhetorical strategy on their part, for if they were to tell us that a certain local congregation is the Christian community that most shapes their views, then our likely reaction would be, "So what?" After all, if there is no essence to Christian language, then their so-called "Christian" language is really just that spoken by a local community. And if there is no essence to language, and language use by local communities makes their world, then that world is just the result of how some specific group of Christians happens to talk. But since we may not be part of that group, why should the rest of us be interested in how they happen to have made their world, when we have made ours according to our own particular language?

But it seems that Hauerwas, Kallenberg, Grenz, and Franke do not want to say that their views are just a matter of how some local, particular congregation or community talks. If that were the case, why would they not just print their books by a publisher or local printer just for their community? No, they want to say much more than just that. They want us to learn to see as they have, which is to see "rightly," and in particular they want us to see that we are on the "inside" of language and cannot get "out." But that insistence, as well as the sweeping, universal character of their claims, should make us think that, instead, they presuppose they have found *the* truth of the matter. But that is possible only if they presuppose that they can get outside of language to reality and know it as it really is.

In chapter 7, we will consider two counterarguments that they might likely offer to this conclusion. First, Grenz and Franke believe that despite our limitations by being so pervasively influenced by language, the Holy Spirit still can give us revelation. Second, they could reply that simply having the Scriptures in common among the various local Christian communities is enough to unite them as being Christian. In the context of issues for Christian theology and ethics, we will return to these two issues. But at this point, let me simply point out that the key issue is that, according to these writers, even if God could bypass the influences of our language, we ourselves cannot escape them, and so any revelation He gives must be interpreted by us in terms of how we use our language. Meaning, they tell us, is primarily a matter of how language is used within a given community, and so we would interpret (and thus construct) the meaning of any revelation by the particular rules and emphases in any given Christian community. If we take their view seriously that there is no essence to language (even Christian language), but there are only languages in particular communities, then the various Christian communities will have their own specific rules and emphases for how they interpret Scripture. *So no matter how well God reveals objective truth to us, we cannot know it as such; we always are on the "inside" of language and therefore we must make for ourselves the meaning of the revelation.* Thus, the prospects for knowing revealed, objective truth are dismal at best.

This kind of problem will beset any approach that takes such a strong view of the internal relationship between language and the world. It does not matter whether it is a *Christian* postmodernist's view, it would just as well apply to a more secular postmodern view. Now let us look at further issues involved with another kind of problem facing Hauerwas, Kallenberg, Grenz, and Franke's view: that of the nature of meaning.

THE ISSUE OF MEANING

We just observed that, according to this postmodern view, we cannot know the meaning of an author. Instead, the meaning of a text is up to the interpretive community. To be consistent, the meaning of Scripture should be treated no differently, so we cannot know what God the Holy Spirit had in mind. But are there more problems with meaning on this postmodern view?

I believe there are. According to this view, meaning mainly is a matter of using terms and expressions in accordance with the way a community has established. Meaning is not primarily based on a first-person point of view, and thus not primarily what a person intended when he or she spoke or acted in a certain way. Instead, it is mainly a social, third-person phenomenon and a matter of behavior, whether verbal or nonverbal.

But is this view right? Is this how we learn to use terms, and is meaning basically a matter of correct behavior? Consider the example of a veterinarian's office that treats pets such as dogs, cats, rabbits, and parrots. How do we know how to use the word "dog" correctly? One explanation could be that we do not use the word "dog" when an owner brings in a rabbit or a cat. I also use "dog" in writing when I fill out a request-for-blood-work form so that the lab knows to check a blood sample for typical dog levels. What seems inescapable is that before I (or anyone else in this scenario) know how to use the word "dog" correctly, I need to *see* that the animal is indeed a dog, and not a cat or rabbit or something else. Somehow, *I* need to see that this animal fulfills the concept of being a dog *before I* can know that this situation calls for the use of the term "dog." And for others to check up on and correct my use of terms, they too must have access to the very animal itself. So, there is a fundamental dependence of our knowledge of proper term use on the first-person perspective, and not that of the social group.

Second, it seems we *must* have access to an unconstructed, objective reality in order for language and its rules to even get started. Consider how social agreement on the rules of correct language use ever gets established in the first place. Somehow, in order for social agreement on the rules of a community's language to take place, people come together, form a social bond, and agree on how terms will be used. According to the postmodern view, language and the meaning of words is basically not a private, first-person matter, based primarily on what a person intended when he or she said or wrote some word(s). Therefore, these individuals, as they come together, insofar as they are individuals, are in a pre-linguistic state. But that must mean for Hauerwas,

Kallenberg, Grenz, and Franke that there must be a state in which individuals can know things *apart* from language. This conclusion, therefore, undermines their core assertion that we are "inside" language and cannot "escape" to know objective reality.

Consider another issue, relating to their claim that meaning is mainly a matter of behavior. If they are right, then behavior is meaningful only within a given community. But that is not necessarily the case, for behavior is *inherently* ambiguous.

To help see this, let us consider two examples. First, in a critique of naturalistic evolution, Alvin Plantinga, a leading Christian philosopher, asks us to consider the example of Paul the hominid. Plantinga wants to show that naturalistic evolution is unconcerned about truth. Instead, what matters for evolution to occur is that creatures survive so that their genes are passed on. Thus, on this theory, just like that of the postmodern view we are considering, the mental states (what I had "in mind") of the person are irrelevant for determining the meaning (or, intentions) of the behavior. Whether or not creatures such as Paul have true beliefs about how to survive is irrelevant. All that matters, even if Paul has wildly implausible beliefs, is that he gets his body in the right place in order to survive. Plantinga explains Paul's behavior and possible thought processes as follows:

> Perhaps Paul very much *likes* the idea of being eaten, but whenever he sees a tiger, always runs off looking for a better prospect, because he thinks it unlikely that the tiger he sees will eat him. This will get his body parts in the right place so far as survival is concerned. . . . Or perhaps he thinks the tiger is a large, friendly, cuddly pussycat and wants to pet it; but he also believes the best way to pet it is to run away from it. Or perhaps he confuses running toward it with running away from it, believing of the action that is really running away from it, that it is running toward it; or perhaps he thinks the tiger is a regularly recurring illusion, and, hoping to keep his weight down, has formed the resolution to run a mile at top speed whenever presented with such an illusion; or perhaps he thinks he is about to take part in a sixteen-hundred-meter race, wants to win, and believes the appearance of the tiger is the starting signal.[4]

---

[4] Alvin Plantinga, *Warrant and Proper Function* (New York: Oxford University Press, 1993), 225-226.

All that matters in Plantinga's story is that Paul gets his body to a place at the right time in order for him to survive and thus become part of the evolutionary process. Thus, there is no intrinsic meaning to Paul's behavior. We may think we understand his behavior, but we can never know for sure. These findings lead to the conclusion that behavior is *inherently* ambiguous. But if that is the case, then Hauerwas, Kallenberg, Grenz, and Franke's view will not make sense. By emphasizing behavior, they will not be able to secure meaning.

Let us consider a second case. Suppose we are members of a specific evangelical Christian community in Redlands, California, in the year 2005. In this community, the members have rules that specify what counts as conversion behavior and thus is evidence that the person truly is saved. Such behavior could include the partaking of communion, the telling of one's story about "receiving Jesus," and the utterance of "yes" when the person is asked whether he or she has ever trusted Jesus as Lord and Savior.

Now, we should grant that these are good outward evidences that the person has understood the meaning of becoming a Christian, and these behaviors also are good, likely indications that the person truly means by them to be a follower of Christ. But if meaning is primarily a matter of use, then it remains an open question whether the person means what everyone else in the community takes him or her to mean. Just as in the case of Paul the hominid, many other possibilities exist. The person could tell a story or partake in the Lord's Supper so that it simply fits the community's expectations, thus faking the conversion testimony. Indeed, the possibilities are virtually endless.

What these illustrations help show, in part, is that meaning cannot be explained primarily as a third-person point of view. The meaning of any outward behavior will always be an open question. That the community's members get it right when they accurately ascribe meaning to a person's action always depends on what that person himself or herself meant by that action, which requires the first-person point of view of the one doing the action. Therefore, Hauerwas, Kallenberg, Grenz, and Franke's view about the meaningfulness of behavior seems quite mistaken.

CONCLUSION

These are but some of the problems that affect postmodern views like those of Hauerwas, Kallenberg, Grenz, and Franke, who accept a close interrelationship of language and world. The problems we have studied so far seem to affect any such view, whether advocated by Christians or not. But there are other, more specific and troublesome issues that arise for Christian theology, ethics, and ministry when believers take this approach. Christianity, its core beliefs, and even God Himself will end up being a construction made by the way Christians talk. I will address these problems in chapter 7. For now, though, let us continue our assessment of our main authors by examining the views of two leaders of the Emerging Church, Brian McLaren and Tony Jones.

"I drive my car and listen to the Christian radio station. . . . There I hear preacher after preacher be so absolutely sure of his bombproof answers and his foolproof biblical interpretations (in spite of the fact that Preacher A at 9:30 A.M. usually contradicts Preacher B at 10:00 A.M. and so on throughout the day). . . . And the more sure he seems, the less I find myself wanting to be a Christian, because on this side of the microphone, antennas, and speaker, life isn't that simple, answers aren't that clear, and nothing is that sure."

BRIAN MCLAREN
A NEW KIND OF CHRISTIAN, XIII

"What was from the beginning, what we have heard, what we have seen with our eyes, what we beheld and our hands handled, concerning the Word of life. . . . These things I have written to you who believe in the name of the Son of God, in order that you may know that you have eternal life."

THE APOSTLE JOHN, 1 JOHN 1:1; 5:13

SIX

CRITIQUING THE EMERGING CHURCH

In chapter 3, I explored the views of two leaders of the Emerging Church, Brian McLaren and Tony Jones. We saw their observations about the broader cultural effects of modernity as well as its effects on the church. We also saw, especially in Jones's work, some indications of the philosophy driving their views. In chapter 5, I scrutinized and found wanting two main philosophical positions held by postmoderns: that (1) we are "inside" language and cannot escape its influences to know an objective reality; and that (2) meaning is primarily a behavioral matter in a linguistically formed community.

In this chapter, I will survey what I think are several strengths of McLaren and Jones's views. Then I will address a few further questions. For one, to what extent are Jones and McLaren's descriptions of modernity, as well as postmodernity, accurate? For another, to what extent have they accurately identified and described the impact of modernity on culture and the church? These are questions about the *descriptive* accuracy of their claims. In part I will contend they actually have mislabeled a key source of the problems they perceive in the church today. I will give a couple of counterexamples, namely my church and my own story, that help show that in key respects they have misdiagnosed the source of the problems.

As a further question, to what extent should Christians accept their proposals, as well as those offered by Hauerwas, Kallenberg, Grenz, Franke, and Murphy, for a "postmodernization" of the faith itself? Would the acceptance of their proposals lead to an *emerging* church, a new kind of way of being a Christian that allows us to venture ahead in faith, to practice faithful devotion and allegiance to Christ in the new emerging culture of postmodernism? Or would it lead to a *submerging* of the church in culture, such that the church ends up being "snookered" and co-opted by it?[1]

SOME KEY CONTRIBUTIONS OF MCLAREN AND JONES

Both McLaren and Jones pinpoint the need for the church to be authentic. Surely they have hit on a crucial matter. Today we face a widespread crisis in our society, as evidenced by an appalling lack of integrity in business, athletics, government and politics, and many more institutions, including the church. McLaren and Jones are in tune with postmoderns and their strong desire to see people live out their values and message, for people to practice what they preach. Surely it is easy for Christians to try to be relevant, all the while being inauthentic, which people can sense so easily today.[2]

Furthermore, they rightly call our attention to the need to live out our faith in community. It is all too easy in our culture to tend to live as an individual believer, and not in close relationships with other Christians. But, scripturally, we need the body of Christ, or else the body (and its members too) will not function as it (and they) should.

I also deeply appreciate their concern to awaken Christians to the need to be missions-minded in order to reach postmoderns. As we move from a modern to a more postmodern culture, we need to understand the mind-sets, values, and even language(s) of postmoderns, just as we would in order to reach any other cross-cultural people group. This is a solid insight based on good missiological principles. In effect, McLaren and Jones are calling Christians to determine how to contextualize the gospel—how it can be presented and lived out in a culture without losing its essential traits.

In light of these valid and helpful emphases in the writings of McLaren and Jones, and because both of them are actively engaged in ministry relationships with postmoderns, we need to contemplate carefully their reports and recommendations for how to reach out to postmoderns. Donald Carson puts this point a bit differently: we need to

---

[1] This is a question raised by D. A. Carson in, "What Is the Real Emerging Church?" Cedarville University, 2004 Staley Lecture Series, February 10, 2004.
[2] D. A. Carson, *Becoming Conversant with the Emerging Church* (Grand Rapids, Mich.: Zondervan, 2005), 49-51.

realize that leaders of the Emerging Church have developed deep concerns for reaching postmodern people, and they also have developed abilities to talk with them; they have learned their language(s).[3] McLaren's various examples in *More Ready Than You Realize* help to illustrate these concerns quite well.

Jones also is correct in recommending the use of stories to help communicate truths to postmodern people. This is one of the most powerful ways to teach truths. I may lecture about a given philosophy, but if I can share a personal illustration to drive home the point, that usually will stick in people's memories. Similarly, if a preacher can illustrate a doctrinal point, maybe metaphorically or by analogy, rather than just expound on it theoretically, people tend to remember and understand it. In doing so, we appeal not just to logos, to reason, but also to pathos, and thus to people's emotions. When we add strong character (ethos) to the mix, our message will be more powerful and credible.

Jones also is right to point out that doctrine affects our experience, and experience affects doctrine. Let me qualify and illustrate that statement. Suppose that a woman becomes a Christian. She comes from an abusive family, in which her father molested her. I imagine it will be rather difficult (to say the least) for her to consider God as her Abba Father, at least until she has had significant time and perhaps much professional help to deal with her deep wounds. Her experience affects her ability to *grasp* doctrine and how she sees God. But on the other hand, if she can grasp God as Abba Father (Rom. 8:15), then that opens up new realms of experience for her, to know His tender lovingkindness as "Daddy." So doctrine also can affect experience.

Here are a few more key strengths McLaren and Jones have to offer, and I do not intend that this list be an exhaustive summary. They call our attention to the desire of postmodern people to experience God, to experience His transcendence, and to find themselves in wonder and awe over who God is. Lately I too have begun down a path that is resulting in far deeper experiences of God than I have known before, and it is wonderful! Finally, I am getting a deep sense of joy over experiencing the freedom (e.g., from the power and pain of sin) I have in Christ. We can easily fall into believing all the right truths, doctrinally speaking, and still not

---

[3] Ibid.

have a deep, vibrant walk with Jesus, which I think McLaren and Jones are right to call us back to. That is, we need to wed together our "heads" and our "hearts," so that we may have a deep, rich walk with Christ. To put it differently, we need to wed together grace and truth.

McLaren also calls us to "a generous orthodoxy," one that will not focus simply on preparing people to live in heaven with God forever, but also to live now as committed followers of Jesus.[4] I think McLaren is calling our attention to something *very* important here. I recall one time when Dallas Willard told me that a particular Christian organization was more concerned about preparing people to die than to live (!), and that echoes exactly what McLaren is trying to say. Being a disciple of Jesus means that I must learn how to follow Him now, in all aspects of my life, including all my days on earth, and McLaren is right to call our attention to that.

Furthermore, McLaren, Jones, and other postmodern believers are sensitive to how we use our language, and the effects that our speech and written words can have on others. So, we should listen when they tell us that among postmoderns, if we talk of "winning" people to Christ, that implies just what they admonish us—that someone will "lose." Or, that if we talk about apologetics as a "defense," then we are fighting with the postmoderns with whom we are talking, and that attitude will come across to them, so that we likely will not influence them positively for the Lord.

As a broad generalization, I found McLaren and Jones's many descriptions of modernity as opposed to postmodernity rather provocative and often quite helpful, at least to begin to engage with their thinking. But it is here that we need to begin to consider just how accurate they are in these descriptions.

MCLAREN AND JONES'S DESCRIPTION OF MODERNITY

There are a couple of main areas in McLaren and Jones's description of modernity on which I want to concentrate. These include, first, their description of foundationalism and the penchant for certainty in our

---

[4] Brian McLaren, *A Generous Orthodoxy* (Grand Rapids, Mich.: Zondervan/Youth Specialties, 2004), 45, 48-49.

knowledge, and second, various descriptions McLaren offers about the modern church.

Their Description of Foundationalism and the Need for Absolute Certainty

Jones and McLaren both think that the church in the West largely has accepted the belief that we must have invincible certainty in our beliefs. There is *some* validity to this claim, but the extent to which we should accept it remains to be seen. Descartes' method of doubting whatever he could, until he could find beliefs he could not doubt, led to a dark period in philosophy. He found that he could doubt most everything, since it was possible he was being deceived by an evil demon. Descartes finally landed upon the realization that he thought, and to be able to think, he had to exist; he could not doubt that—or so he reasoned.

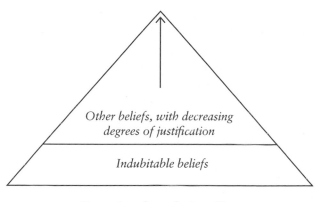

Other beliefs, with decreasing degrees of justification

Indubitable beliefs

Cartesian foundationalism

Descartes' project was an attempt to find an unshakeable foundation for knowledge, one that could not be defeated by skeptical claims. If there is a kind of foundationalism that matches well with what McLaren, Jones, and our other authors criticize, this is it. There are a few problems with both Descartes' foundationalism itself and McLaren and Jones's description of foundationalism. Let me tackle these two issues in turn.

Descartes' foundationalism: First, to require that our beliefs be indubitable, certain, and "bombproof," in order to count as knowledge, is an *extremely* unrealistic standard, and skeptics know it. A skeptic, such as David Hume, could always reply, "But isn't it just *possible* [no matter how unlikely, I might interject] that you *could* be mistaken?" If we are at all honest with ourselves, we would answer yes, but then the skeptic has us right where he or she wants us, if we hold to Descartes' certainty standard.

Does this mean the skeptic wins? How should we deal with the skeptic? If we assert that we know that we aren't being deceived by an evil demon because we know we ate breakfast this morning, the skeptic can reply by demanding a criterion for how we know that further thing: "But, how do you know that? Surely you *could* be deceived on that matter, *couldn't* you?" If we take that bait and play by the skeptic's own rules, we are doomed, for the skeptic can keep demanding a criterion for how we can know anything, so that we can't ever get started and know *anything!*

The answer to skeptics, therefore, is not to play their game on their terms (which can be called *epistemic methodism*, the view that we must have a criterion to know anything). Instead, there are some things we simply know, without having to provide a criterion to anyone else to show how we know them. For example, I simply know that I am married to Debbie, that 2+2=4, that red is a color, that murder is wrong, and many more such things. There are particular things I simply do know (which approach is called *epistemic particularism*), and now the burden is on the skeptic to defeat my claim to know these things. In this strategy, I simply *rebut* the skeptical assertions; I don't have to feel the additional burden of *proving* him or her to be wrong (i.e., I do not have to *refute* the skeptic). Notice that my knowledge claims do not require "bombproof" certainty.

So much for dealing with skepticism. But it is true that Descartes' approach tended to play into a skeptic's hands. The myth of having to have "bombproof" answers to challengers is an unfortunate holdover from his influence. While we do not have to have certainty to know things, Descartes' legacy still has had its effects, in the church as much as in the broader culture.

McLaren and Jones's description of foundationalism: As the second issue, let us now turn to McLaren and Jones's description of foundationalism. It is clear that they think of foundationalism as the Cartesian variety. There are, however, other kinds of foundationalism. Foundationalism as a philosophical view is far from dead today, despite protestations to the contrary. It still is alive and well, according to philosophers like Michael DePaul (see chapter 3, note 90), Laurence BonJour, and Paul Moser.[5]

Not only is foundationalism far from dead, I do not know of any living philosopher who thinks we must have certainty in our foundational beliefs. Quite simply, the portrayal of foundationalism as requiring certainty in the basic, foundational beliefs is a caricature of the view. People realize that the certitude requirement is ridiculously high as a standard for having knowledge. I have already pointed out various counters to this position as part of my rebuttal against skepticism. There are several things we know, yet without certainty. Here are but a few examples. I *know* that George W. Bush is the forty-third president of the United States, but do I know this with invincible certainty? No; I could be mistaken, although I highly doubt it (your evidence to show me I am wrong would have to be extremely compelling). I *know* that rape is wrong, with about as much confidence as any belief may have. That belief seems as close to certain as beliefs may get. I also know that I now work for Biola University, that I used to live in Moraga, California, and that I married my wife on October 27, 1984. I know that terrorists attacked the United States on September 11, 2001. Could I be mistaken about these things? Logically speaking, it is *conceivable* that I could be mistaken. It *might* be the case that some mad scientist is deceiving me

---

[5] Moser and BonJour are leading epistemologists. Moser discusses the structure of justification, that there cannot be an endless regress, or chain, of beliefs. A set of beliefs must begin somewhere in terms of its justification. "If this is right [i.e., his foregoing assessment of how our beliefs are structured], the structure of justification does not involve circles, endless regresses, or unjustified starter-beliefs. That is, this structure is evidently foundationalist. . . . Given appropriate flesh, and due attention to skepticism about justification, this [regress] argument poses a serious challenge to non-foundationalist accounts of the structure of epistemic justification, such as epistemic coherentism. More significantly, foundationalism will then show forth as *one of the most compelling accounts of the structure of knowledge and justification. This explains, at least in part, why foundationalism has been very prominent historically and is still widely held in contemporary epistemology*" (Paul K. Moser, "Foundationalism," in *The Cambridge Dictionary of Philosophy*, 2nd ed., ed. Robert Audi [Cambridge: Cambridge University Press, 1999], 323 [emphasis mine]).

BonJour reasons that it "is doubtful that there is any very general agreement concerning the deficiencies of foundationalism; indeed, many of those who reject it do not seem to have any very definite argument in mind. Thus, as happens with rather alarming frequency in philosophy, *the movement away from foundationalism in the last three decades or so often looks less like a reasoned dialectical progression than a fashionable stampede*" (Laurence BonJour, "The Dialectic of Foundationalism and Coherentism," *The Blackwell Guide to Epistemology*, ed. John Greco and Ernest Sosa [Oxford: Blackwell, 1999], 120 [emphasis mine]).

with drugs, or maybe some other wild story might be true. But why should I believe these mere possibilities? I am entitled to my knowledge claims, even if I do not hold them with "bombproof," one hundred percent certainty. I need good and sufficient evidence to believe that I am mistaken, over and against my other, much more highly justified beliefs. I want to believe as many truths as possible, and disbelieve as many falsehoods as possible, too. In that process, I may make some mistakes. But if I do not have one hundred percent certainty, why would that mean that I do not know many things?

To reiterate, to require certainty is a ridiculous and unjustifiable standard for knowledge. But many, if not most, philosophers today are foundationalists. So something is wrong in McLaren and Jones's description of foundationalism and a "modern" view of what is required for knowledge. Foundationalist philosophers today have adopted a more modest foundationalism, one that does not require certainty in the foundational beliefs.

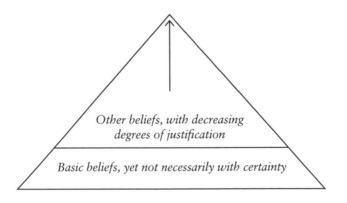

Other beliefs, with decreasing degrees of justification

Basic beliefs, yet not necessarily with certainty

A more modest foundationalism

Let us also look at the standard definition of knowledge, to see that certainty is not necessary for knowledge. I may form beliefs on a great many subjects. For instance, I may see a few people walking on a short stretch on the beach boardwalk with ice cream cones and therefore form a belief that there is an ice cream store nearby. I believe this. That is, I accept the proposition that an ice cream store is nearby. Does my belief require that I also know it to be the case? No. I believe that there is an ice cream store nearby, but that could be false; maybe they all had dessert together at a home and decided to go for a walk.

Traditionally, philosophers have understood knowledge to have three components. That is, knowledge is *justified true belief*. First, we must *believe* something (that is, we accept a proposition, like the proposition that there is an ice cream store nearby), or else we cannot know it.

Second, the belief must be *justified*. That is, there must be *sufficient* evidence for a person to affirm (accept) that proposition, in which case it is justified. Obviously, this quality comes in degrees. If it were the case that *all* these ice cream cones had wrappers on them with the words "Dairy Queen," then it would seem more likely that my belief is justified. Suppose also there is a sign ahead that says "Dairy Queen." Then my belief has much more evidence to support (and hence justify) it.

The level of justification needed for there to be knowledge may also vary by person. For instance, some of those people with a cone might have additional evidence (namely, they made their ice cream cones at a house) that is not available to me. Suppose there is evidence available to someone else, but not to me, that would count against my belief that there is an ice cream store nearby. In that case—if that evidence remains unknown to me—then my belief (that there is an ice cream store nearby) may remain justified for me but it would not be a justified belief for the person who is eating the cone that he knows was made at the home.

So not everyone may have the same amount, or even the same kind, of evidence for a belief. Also, the weight of the evidence in support of a belief may change over time as new evidence is considered. Justification typically is defeasible, although some beliefs' justification may be exceedingly hard to overturn (such as in the cases that murder is wrong, and that 2+2=4).

As an illustration, consider the nature of the burden of proof in legal cases. In most civil cases, the standard for the quantity (or level) of proof required to convict is a *preponderance of the evidence*. That is, "the truth of the fact asserted is more likely true than not."[6] But in most crim-

---

[6] I am indebted to the insights of Kevin Lewis, J.D., Th.M., my Biola colleague, who made these observations to me in e-mail correspondence, August 10, 2004.

inal cases, the level of proof required is higher. The jury must be convinced *beyond a reasonable doubt* that the fact in question is true. So, there is a much higher standard of justification to convict in criminal cases than in civil ones, and this burden of proof reflects the more serious nature of the charges.

How does this assessment apply to the justification of theological beliefs, for instance, that Jesus rose from the dead? There can be much evidence in support of the bodily resurrection available to people to examine, but there also are arguments against it offered by critics, such as the scholars who have come to be known as the "Jesus Seminar." Suppose someone believes that Jesus rose from the dead. This belief can be justified for that person by evidence like the internal conviction of the Holy Spirit, even if that evidence may be difficult to communicate in a compelling way to a skeptic. Suppose this person's belief is shaken when confronted by a secular professor, who challenges his evidence for belief by claiming that science has shown that dead people do not rise. It is possible that this Christian's degree of justification could be lessened by this challenge, but there also is much more evidence available, such as from the arguments offered by William Lane Craig, Gary Habermas, N. T. Wright, and others.[7] So, this person's degree of justification could increase upon the examination of further evidence.

So beliefs can have degrees of justification, and the amount of justification a belief may enjoy may vary over time, due to a variety of influences on our assessment of the evidence (such as more cognitive material to process, or very painful circumstances from our past). Roderick Chisholm has classified a scale of these degrees of justification:

6. Certain
5. Obvious
4. Evident
3. Beyond reasonable doubt
2. Epistemically in the clear
1. Probable
0. Counterbalanced (the evidence for and against offset each other)

---

[7] I list some resources in general apologetics in the bibliography.

-1. Probably false
-2. In the clear to disbelieve
-3. Reasonable to disbelieve
-4. Evidently false
-5. Obviously false
-6. Certainly false[8]

Degrees 1 to 6 are degrees of *positive epistemic status* (i.e., the degree to which a belief enjoys justification in favor of its acceptance; that justification can range from a low degree to a high degree). Conversely, from -1 to -6, beliefs may have a negative degree of justification, due to reasons why we should not accept them, and these degrees also reflect increasing degrees of evidence against that belief. So, I can have beliefs that are not justified and thus do not count as knowledge.

Now let us consider the third condition for knowledge: that the belief is *true*. Since I am describing the traditional "tripartite" definition of knowledge ("justified true belief"), let me continue in that same vein with the traditional definition of truth, which is that a proposition is true if it corresponds to reality. For example, it is true that O. J. Simpson was acquitted of the charge of murdering his wife Nicole; that is the way things turned out in reality. It is false that Al Gore is the forty-third president of the United States, since he did not win the election. So truth, at least as traditionally conceived, and as we often use the term in ordinary language, means that a proposition matches up with reality.

I can hold beliefs that may be justified (on the basis of the evidence available to me) and that I believe are true, but I may realize later that they are false, in light of new evidence. This was the case with theories about what is involved with combustion. People used to believe that a substance called phlogiston was key to combustion, but that view later was replaced with oxygen theory. The people who believed the phlogiston theory about fire were entitled to claim that they had knowledge when they believed the phlogiston theory, even if they did not know *for certain* whether or not that belief was true. The evidence (i.e., the justification) for affirming and holding a belief is just that—evidence—and we may find out later, upon further examination, that some theory is

---

[8] Roderick M. Chisholm, *Theory of Knowledge*, 3rd ed., *Foundations of Philosophy Series* (Englewood Cliffs, N.J.: Prentice Hall, 1989), 16.

mistaken, or that a convicted person is innocent, or that we were mistaken in some particular knowledge claim.

Therefore it simply is not the case that according to foundationalism we *must* have certainty in our beliefs. We can hold beliefs that count as knowledge even without that high a standard of justification. Also, a belief's justification often can be defeated. We may affirm (accept) that a belief is true, and yet we may find evidence later that it is false. Certainty is just not required. In that respect, McLaren, Jones, and others we have looked at are inaccurate in their description of foundationalism. There is ample room for humility in our knowledge claims, and yet we still can grasp and know foundational truths about the real world.

This claim brings us back to a crucial issue. Recall that the core contention of our postmodern authors regarding foundationalism concerns our supposed inability to have epistemic access to the real, objective world. Jones claims that we *cannot* be objective,[9] since for him we all have our biases and subjectivity. There simply is no neutral place to stand to interpret any event, any text, etc. We cannot get past our backgrounds, perspectives, and our historically situated, conditioned experiences. That, I argued, is the main reason why postmodernists reject foundationalism.

But in the previous chapter I argued that, philosophically, our postmodern authors presuppose this very access to know the real world even though they deny it. Furthermore, I already have suggested a few ways that we do indeed have access to the real world, and in chapter 9 I will unpack that idea in much more detail. Since the point of contention over foundationalism ultimately revolves around the issue of access, which we can and do have, these postmodern, philosophical critiques of foundationalism are mistaken. Furthermore, how does Jones intend for us to understand his claim that objectivity is unattainable? It surely seems he wants us to see how things *really* are, and not just according to how he and his particular community members have constructed their world.

At this point, however, we should heed Jones's caution which I had mentioned in chapter 3. That is, from his perspective, the problem with foundationalism is not with what philosophers believe, for Jones real-

---

[9] E.g., see Tony Jones, *Postmodern Youth Ministry* (Grand Rapids, Mich.: Zondervan/Youth Specialties, 2001), 74 ("no one . . . objectively approaches a text").

izes that in philosophy, foundationalism is far from dead. Instead, as a pastor, he thinks the problem is with the way pastors act, teach, and preach as though they had invincible certainty. Jones feels that such attitudes and actions "put off" many "seekers."

This is an important counterargument to my view, so let us consider it carefully. I think *for the sake of argument* we can grant Jones that many pastors do act and behave in these ways. I will be quick to admit, however, that this is not the case at my church, which I will describe below in more detail. But again, for the sake of argument, let us grant Jones's observation. In the current cultural climate, I see how these attitudes would turn off postmoderns. But *must* such pastors carry an attitude of invincible certainty in their beliefs in the truth of Christianity and its teachings? Or, *should* they?

I believe that the evidence for Christianity is overwhelmingly in favor of its being the truth. But on my account of modest foundationalism above, we need not have *certainty* in our beliefs in order to *know* that they are true. Indeed, there are precious few things we may know with certainty without even the *possibility* of being mistaken (recall how we need to just rebut, and not refute, the skeptic). Does this preclude us from having great confidence and much, much justification for our beliefs in the truth of Christianity? Not at all. We can and should hold our beliefs with humility, for at least a couple of reasons: (1) we could possibly be mistaken (yet, we may not know of any sufficient reason why we should *not* be confident that we have the truth), and (2) we realize that we can turn off people whose culture has taught them to be suspicious of those who claim to have objective truth.

Note again that my form of modest foundationalism has much, much room for humility; one can be a foundationalist and yet be humble in one's claims. For instance, as believers, we should be confident that we have the truth in the authoritative, inerrant Word of God. Yet that doesn't mean that we hold all our Christian beliefs with an equally high degree of justification. For instance, I think the evidence is overwhelmingly in favor of our holding to the belief that Jesus literally, bodily rose from the dead. That is a justified true belief. But that belief has more evidence in its favor than does, say, a belief that the pre-Tribulation Rapture theory is true. Theoretically, it is possible we could be mistaken in some interpretations, as well as applications, of Scripture, but others are so clear that we have no good reason to doubt them. In short, therefore, I do not see Jones's rejoinder as defeating my argument for a more modest foundationalism.

However, I should counterbalance what I have just written with another important realization. So far, I have been discussing humility in the sense that we need not have certainty in our beliefs in order to know. That is, we *might* be mistaken. But there is another sense to our use of the term "humility." Jesus was not mistaken; indeed, He knew with certainty that He is the Son of God, and yet He was humble in how He expressed this and other truths. He was not arrogant; He presented objective truth, which He knew with certainty, in a winsome manner. The apostle Paul likewise wrote his letters with an air of certainty in his claims about who Jesus is. But he also wrote with great humility. So, being humble does not necessarily entail being less than certain. Humility also involves our presenting and living truth in winsome ways rather than with arrogance or condescension. Some Christians do take this latter attitude, and that is a serious problem.[10]

Carson also offers a helpful way to assess McLaren and Jones's description of modernity and the certainty requirement for knowledge. He says that Emerging Church leaders seem to present us with a false antithesis, namely, that either we know something with certainty (that is, with omniscience), or else we are left with uncertainty. Now, from my previous discussion, we should see that this is a false dichotomy, that we may know many things without certainty.

Even so, let us consider from a biblical standpoint whether we must have omniscience in order to know things. Carson calls us to consider the way biblical authors wrote. For instance, they frequently appeal with confidence to truths that they know, that they are sure of (for instance, John's account of his eyewitness encounters with Jesus in 1 John 1:1-3); or, that unless we believe certain truths (for example, that Jesus is the Christ), particular results will follow (we will not see the kingdom of heaven). Did these writers need omniscience in order to know these truths? Clearly, no.[11]

Before we leave this topic, let me make a further distinction between

---

[10] I am grateful to Justin Taylor for these and other insightful comments on a draft of this chapter.
[11] See Carson, *Becoming Conversant with the Emerging Church,* 193-200.

the status of the *object* of our belief, and our belief *itself,* and its justification. The Bible is God's Word, and *what it is* does not depend upon *my confidence in its being so.* They are two entirely different things. While my confidence in my belief in the Bible's status may vary (as it did when I was a new Christian), that does not affect the status of what the Bible is in itself. The Bible is what it is, whether or not I have utter certainty in my belief about it, or even if I am certain that it is false (to appeal to two extremes on Chisholm's scale).

Their description of modernity's influence on the church: If McLaren and Jones's description of modernity is faulty—and it is—then that may have other implications. We should examine just what it is McLaren and Jones are describing and finding at fault, to see if these characteristics really are due to modernity's influences, or if they are due to something quite different. To do this, let us recall several claims of how modernity has impacted the church, and here I will focus on what McLaren has to say.

McLaren says that modern Christians are controlling and not compassionate. They are Pharisaical, legalistic, arrogant, rigid, and uptight, and they want to keep things safe doctrinally and avoid heresy. Furthermore, they want salvation and the Christian life pinned down to nice, neat categories and simple formulas. The transmission of information, rather than the transformation of people, becomes the focus of discipleship. But these approaches lead to tremendous internal struggles when we face problems that resist such explanations and approaches, says McLaren, for there are no new insights beyond such formulas. In the cases of people with such problems, their problems are compounded because there are no people with whom they can open up. Their questions or doubts cannot be examined, if we must have absolute certainty in our beliefs. We put ourselves in a very restrictive box, and when life becomes messy and we hurt and struggle, we can end up in a crisis of faith, much like what McLaren himself experienced. Furthermore, Christians tend to treat dogmas as free-floating abstractions, and by trying to figure out all of life by means of neat, tidy categories, they by and large lose their sense of wonder over who God is.

Now, to what extent are these situations the result of modernity? Or, are there other possible explanations? Carson suggests that leaders of the Emerging Church, such as McLaren, actually are reacting to their particular, conservative Christian backgrounds,[12] and that they unjustifiably generalize from their own experiences to the whole church in the West, concluding that the church's problems are a result of modernity's influences.[13]

I believe we can see if modernity is the prime culprit in these problems by asking if we must embrace a "new way" (i.e., a postmodern way) of being a Christian in order to address these issues. I think the answer clearly will be no. Let us consider some cases, to see if my suggested answer follows.

Case # 1—A church case study: First, consider the case of my particular church, Trinity Evangelical Free Church in Redlands, California. Trinity has a wide variety of members and attenders, including young and old, several international students, and many professional people with advanced college degrees who work as doctors, educators, business people, lawyers, and so forth. We are growing more and more as a missions-minded church, both in our local community and abroad. We are trying to show the love of Christ by acts of service locally by taking time and effort to assist and improve local schools, as well as train people who need computer skills to get jobs. We also serve disadvantaged families by providing a place for kids to come and see the love and care of Christians as they minister to the needs of the whole person.

Furthermore, at Trinity, we emphasize community, realizing that people can feel quite lost in the large Sunday morning services. We have established several ways for people to find fellowship in the context of a small group. My wife and I have participated in such groups for several years now, and this has been a main way we have formed deeper relationships among committed, caring Christians. For example, our small group rallied behind us when we became parents, throwing a baby shower, lending a crib, providing meals, and offering helpful advice.

One of our church's ministries is called Pathways. It is a system of support groups for people facing all kinds of trials or struggles. We have groups for people struggling with divorce, homosexuality, sexual abuse, and more. In this kind of group, we aim to show God's compassion to people, and we do not try to fix people's complex wounds by application

---

[12] Ibid., 85-86.
[13] D. A. Carson, "Evaluating a Complex Movement," Cedarville University, 2004 Staley Lectures, February 11, 2004.

of simple formulas. Also in Pathways, as well as in other kinds of small groups, we recognize that some people want to "come and see" the reality of our faith by how we live, so we will encourage people who are not members or even attenders of Trinity to be a part of a small group.

Our services are very worshipful in music, dance, drama, and preaching. Classes are offered on a variety of topics to help people understand core Christian beliefs. Other classes include missionary prayer, contemporary ethical topics, and apologetics. At Trinity, we believe in the inerrancy and authority of Scripture, that there is objective truth, and that it has been revealed in special and general revelation. Nowhere else have I heard preaching that exhibits such a high view of Scripture as the infallible, inerrant, authoritative Word of God but that also integrates insights from other disciplines, such as philosophy, in a very coherent Christian worldview. Does that mean that we must have certainty in our beliefs? No. But we do believe that we have the truth given in Scripture and that we can faithfully exposit and interpret Scripture and make it relevant and applicable to all aspects of life. My pastors exhibit humility, all the while holding fast to their belief that we have the foundational truth in Scripture.

In sum, my church stands in stark contrast to McLaren's descriptions of a typical modern evangelical church. Clearly, we believe that there is objective truth and we can know it, and that Scripture provides the foundation for truth. But we do not require that people believe it without even the possibility of doubt. Rather, we think that the evidence for scriptural teachings is so great that we ought to accept them, even if it is possible that someone may doubt them. In other words, we have a very robust confidence in the truth of the Bible as God's Word, but we do not need certainty to know that. Now, McLaren might object that my church is the exception to his general rule, but I think this example shows that churches can thrive and not be postmodern as he expects. Nor must they be modern as he expects in order to thrive. There can be strong, biblically thriving churches in a postmodern age that do not fit his modern and postmodern categories, and I think my church is not alone.[14]

Also, our pastoral staff, as well as other leaders, model a view of the

---

[14] As but one more example, Carson also describes such a church in New York in *Becoming Conversant with the Emerging Church*, 56.

Christian life that is not as simplistic as McLaren's portrayal. Living the Christian life is far more complex than applying just a system of simple formulas, which is why we have Pathways groups. We realize that there are important insights to be gained from good psychology, good philosophy, and more.

Also, contrary to McLaren, we do not try to simplify life down to a system of inputs and outputs, which is how some approaches to discipleship could be understood ("If I just pray, read the Bible, attend church, witness, and am filled with the Spirit, I will have love, joy, peace, and all the other fruit of the Spirit in my life"). Such approaches can be understood to treat the Christian life as all *my* responsibility to do these steps right. If I am not experiencing these qualities, then something is wrong with me (my sin, usually). If it is my fault, I need to confess and get right with God and obey. But we recognize that there also are other factors that can impede our ability to experience the fruit of the Spirit.

My church strikes me as an anomaly for McLaren's view. Trinity is not a church that has rejected foundationalism, and we do not require certainty in our beliefs, yet we do not have the "corrosive" problems that supposedly mark modern churches. And yet, we have not become a postmodern church. We aim for being deeply authentic people who can talk with all segments of society.

Case # 2—McLaren's story, and mine: As we have seen, in his own life, McLaren has had to personally grapple with several pressures, one of which was the notion that he had to have bombproof certainty in his beliefs. He also learned and experienced a controlling, legalistic view of the Christian life. He was taught that the Christian life could be treated as the application of formulas. But when he had questions or doubts, he was not able to find "safe" believers with whom he could be vulnerable. These problems and pressures, he concluded, are due to interpreting Christianity in a modern way, whereas the solution to them is found in embracing a new, postmodern way of being a Christian.

Now, let us consider my own story, in light of McLaren's story and as a second counterexample to McLaren and Jones's description of modernism's influence on the church. God blessed me with wonderful parents who deeply loved me, and I dearly love them. When each one passed away, those were some of the hardest and saddest times I have experienced, for I had to say goodbye (for now, until I see them again in heaven) to two of the people closest to me. They modeled many good qualities for me, such as their deep love for each other, their Christian commitment, their good character, their hard work and desire to use their God-given talents, and their love for our extended family.

My parents were born in the early days of the fundamentalist movement. My dad's father was a first-generation Nazarene minister, so my dad's early life was one of strict obedience. It was strongly perfectionistic, and salvation was never seen as certain. My folks were married amid the Great Depression, and that profoundly shaped their values as well.

I was born about a year later than Brian McLaren. My family attended church every Sunday, and I heard the gospel early in life. I remember being granted "release time" from my public elementary school classes in order to go to a trailer parked on the street, where a few others and I received Bible instruction. I grew up knowing about God, knowing that I was a sinner, and that Jesus died for my sins.

But I also grew up with some of the same anxieties my folks had experienced. I thought that I had to prove my value by being perfect, or else risk rejection. Somehow as a young child I must have projected that fear onto God, too, for I would constantly confess my sins under my breath, even when playing with a friend.

We moved from my childhood home in southern California when I was nearly eleven years old, and that started a process that eventually led me to receive Jesus as my Savior and Lord. I had a hard time making friends in the new area, and was very lonely. But I wanted to fit in and be accepted, and over time, I realized that I would need to go against some of my family's values in order to be accepted by my peers.

At age twenty, I became infatuated with a young lady at college. But the relationship was rocky. I really tried to make it work, but as the relationship with her went up and down, I felt my own sense of worth and acceptance going up and down too.

At church, I started listening to the sermons more carefully. I discovered a version of the New Testament called *The Greatest Is Love* and read 1 Corinthians 13, which was reprinted on the back cover, to compare my feelings and attitudes toward this girl with God's standard. I realized how far short of God's standards I was falling. But I also came to realize that God loved me and offered me a relationship with Him through His Son. I had not understood that part before—that I myself had to do something about Jesus—but one night in late April 1978, I knelt down next to my bed, and through many tears, asked Jesus into my life.

A few months later, Steve, a Christian at college, followed up with me, and I began to grow as a new believer. But after about a year, I went through a severe time of doubting. I had told two of my political science professors that I had become a Christian, and they challenged me with questions about the rationality of my newfound faith, questions that shook me deeply.

I was afraid that maybe what I had believed all my life might not be true, and as I talked with my discipler-friend, Steve, he would try to help, but I still feared that I could be mistaken. I eventually found Josh McDowell's *Evidence That Demands a Verdict* and *More Evidence That Demands a Verdict*, and those books were immensely helpful. Despite learning many new lines of evidence in support of my belief, however, I still had doubts. I worried about the truth of Christianity, even though I now knew better intellectually. I would keep reminding myself of the facts, but they did not remove my fears.

Now I can look back on those days of doubt and understand more clearly what was going on. At the time, I did not understand Romans 7, that even though I had become a Christian, I still had the "old man," who would resist the Spirit. I also still felt that I had to be perfect before God, that I had to be perfect even in my belief, or else God would not accept me.

Notice, then, that I experienced something like what McLaren describes: I thought I had to be certain in my faith, without any room for fear or doubt. But that was not something I had learned from reading the Bible; rather, in my case, it largely was from my own fear that I had to prove my value before God and others by being perfect. That kind of fear can be paralyzing. The kind of control I needed over my life (including every uttered or written word, every fleeting thought, or every sudden feeling) to try to keep up that standard was enormous and overwhelming, and it manifested itself in various ways, such as the belief that I *had* to have daily devotions. I became pretty rigid as a Christian, all out of fear that I had to measure up to God's perfection, lest He reject me. These fears surfaced to my awareness from time to time, even though I could quote to you Bible passages about how we are saved by grace through faith, which is not of ourselves but is God's gift. It was as though I knew the truth of Scripture but deep down in my soul was prevented from experiencing the joy of being a Christian.

I had joined a Christian organization to help spread the gospel. I was taught, much as McLaren was, that I could share my faith using a gospel tract, and I also learned how to grow as a Christian by learning to be filled with the Spirit and surrender control of my life to Christ. I practiced with great energy the disciplines of faith, whether that be praying, reading and memorizing Scripture, witnessing, thanking God, confessing my sins (which I did often!), or asking God to be Lord of my life. But I did not have much joy. Yes, I was seeing God move in my life, answering prayers and using me in His service, and I was seeing Him work in powerful ways (such as in Zaire during one summer outreach).

God also brought a special young lady into my life as my next-door neighbor, who later became my wife. At the time I met Debbie, I was aware of being quite lonely, and a counselor had told me that, since God had pointed out that need in my life, He must be ready to meet it. Now, that pronouncement was both exciting and scary! I knew it meant I would have to be vulnerable, and the prospect of facing rejection was scary.

Debbie and I dated off and on for two years, and we grew closer together through many events, like our serving in short-term missions. Here too, however, I struggled with fears—in this case, fears that she would break off our engagement unless I was perfect.

Furthermore, while growing up, I had learned that it is sin to be angry. It was not okay to experience such feelings, or any other "negative" ones. This hindered me in knowing and expressing how I felt, and often I suppressed hurt or anger, thinking that as a good Christian I just shouldn't have such struggles. After all, I reasoned, all I had to do was confess my sin and let the Spirit be in charge of my life, and then I should experience God's joy. But I did not experience such joy consistently.

Many people I worked with, though not all, held those attitudes, namely, that there were two sources of the problems in life: (a) physical ones, and (b) spiritual ones. Physical problems were due to illness, accidents, and the like. But spiritual problems were thought to be of one main source—sin, and in particular, *my* sin. If I were to do all the right things that a good disciple would do, especially if I would confess my sin, then I could experience God's joy. But why was I not experiencing it? Why was I so bound up with fear and anxiety?

The beginning of an answer came with a simple realization. Yes, in general, sin is the root cause of our problems as human beings, but we have experienced not only the impact of our own sin but also *the effects of others' sins against us.* We all live in a fallen world, and we know that we experience the effects of sin and sinful actions, but all too easily in evangelical circles we can discount the depth of the impact of others' actions against us. It is as though in some circles we believe that *all* we need to do is practice the right spiritual disciplines, and then the fruit of the Spirit should be manifested in our lives in increasing measure—the right inputs yield the right outputs.

So I, like McLaren, hit roadblocks where I could not make sense of my experience in light of my *expectations* of the Christian life, which came from a certain kind of conservative, evangelical perspective. I could not reduce the Christian life to just a formulaic approach.

The Christian organization in which I worked at the time emphasized submission to leadership, often, I believe, at the expense of accountability to God for one's own choices. This issue came to a head for me when I was seriously thinking that God was leading me into a different way to serve Him, by studying at the graduate level how to "defend" the faith. At the same time, there was a powerful, in some ways not-so-subtle message that I should stay with this organization and continue to serve in an administrative role, for those gifts were the ones I had most developed up to that time.

There were powerful dynamics at work to stay with the organization, and in that context, I experienced very strongly what McLaren observes, namely, that evangelicals can be very controlling. With the support of key friends, my wife and I made a very hard decision: I would continue down the graduate school path, and see if God would continue to confirm His leading.

That leading brought me into the path of several mature Christians at a conservative evangelical seminary, Talbot School of Theology. I came there to be mentored by J. P. Moreland and to get good grounding in my theology and philosophy before going on to further graduate work. It was during my time at Talbot, with Moreland and other professors, that I experienced a new kind of Christianity, but not one that was postmodern. I saw how these people were deeply committed to Christ, to the inerrancy and authority of Scripture, to the reality of objective truth and our ability to know it, yet without requiring certainty. I found that these people were *real* human beings; while they loved Jesus deeply and held to these commitments, they were anything but rigid or controlling. They did not see the Christian life as just the proper application of formulas, for they too had suffered and had experienced brokenness, just as I was experiencing. They believed they knew the truth, but they were not anxious about warding off heresy behind every bush, or being legalistic. They did not want to just transmit information; they wanted to impart their very lives to me, to help me grow. They also had a high view of the majesty and greatness of God. They were modest foundationalists in their epistemology, and they did not think they had to have bombproof certainty in their beliefs. And they had a regular, deep, rich experience of the Lord and His presence in the community of the saints.

How could these things be so? How could they exhibit the very opposite traits than the ones McLaren says mark those who believe in foundationalism and knowledge of objective truth? How could their lives be so refreshingly different from what I had experienced up to that time as a Christian? How did they know joy as an ongoing reality of their Christian lives while I didn't? Talbot provided an environment that encouraged us to examine our doubts and questions, to feel free to raise them in a safe place where we could discuss them openly. We looked at many kinds of evidence for our faith, including theological, philosophical, and historical. We also studied carefully what antagonists to the faith had to say. What I found was that there is an abundance of support for the rationality of our belief in Christianity as objectively true, against all kinds of opponents. I also learned that my belief did not have to be certain in order to still count as knowledge.

What marked the lives of my Talbot Seminary professors, if they had not become "new," postmodern kinds of Christians? One major distinguishing trait was this: they knew the reality and truth of God's grace in their lives. They lived in a way that showed that they understood, deeply in their souls, that they were saved by grace, so that they were no longer living under the law. They wed together grace and truth. Thus they could experience God's joy, as well as His sweet presence, in their lives.

Before we go further, we need to stop and take notice that McLaren has put his finger on some traits of how conservative or evangelical Christianity has been practiced, and that quite arguably those practices have been influenced by the traits he has identified of the modern period. Furthermore, these traits have caused considerable confusion and even pain among committed Christians. For instance, I remember how, after presenting some of McLaren's views at an evangelical church, I spoke with a fellow who had worked for the same Christian organization as I had. He said that when he read through *A New Kind of Christian*, he felt that McLaren had pinpointed the very (painful) issues he had been struggling with in terms of how we had been taught to live the Christian life. I don't think he is alone; *McLaren is onto something* in terms of our expectations of living out the Christian life, like our needing to have certainty in our beliefs, believing that if we have doubts, *there is something wrong with us*. That attitude does lead to becoming rigid and controlling (of what we ourselves and others believe and think). Or, if we are struggling in the Christian life, primarily (apart from spiritual warfare) it is due to our own sin and our lack of dealing with it. Or, if we just do all the right things by way of "input" (spiritual disciplines, treated as formulas), then the right "outputs" (the fruit of the Spirit) *definitely* will follow. If they do not, then it is our fault. This is a rigid, formulaic approach to Christianity, not a joyful, grace-filled one, for it puts the burden on the Christian to be sure he or she does everything just right—or else.

Let us now reconsider McLaren's own story. Much like his character Dan Poole, McLaren struggled with many of the same kinds of matters with which I struggled: the pressure to have certainty in his beliefs; the controlling attitudes of fellow believers; a rigid and legalistic approach to the Christian life; the treatment of the Christian life as a simple formula; the understanding of spiritual formation as the proper application of "inputs" (spiritual disciplines, expressed as formulas), without room for doubts, anxieties, and the like; and the lack of safe people with whom he could open up and share his struggles. In McLaren's narrative, Neo diagnoses Dan's problems as being due to a modern way of being a Christian, and his solution is to learn how to be a new, postmodern kind of Christian.

Yet, in juxtaposition to McLaren's story, the diagnosis of my problems is not that I needed to give up foundationalism, or knowledge of objective truth. The struggles I have faced were due to my own woundedness, as well as anxieties I "caught" early in life, coupled with my own responses to them and my fears, misbeliefs, and expectations about having to prove my value or else face rejection. They also were due to my legalistic way of understanding the Christian life. In my case, what were the solutions? They were: (1) healing at the emotional level of my wounds; (2) separating the view of God I grew up with from what God really is like; (3) being able to experience my feelings, even those that are "negative," so that I don't suppress them; and (4) grasping more at the heart level that God really has placed me in the grace in which I stand (Rom. 5:2). The realization and embodiment of these four factors has freed me to experience much more deeply than ever the wonder and joy of God's person, as well as deep, overflowing joy in response to what he has done for me. My ability to have deep, rich experience of God and His presence, especially as Abba, has grown tremendously, and that overflows regularly in deep, heartfelt worship.

God also gifted me with a wonderful wife, that "girl next door," who embodies grace and acceptance to me, thus helping me understand unconditional love. Notice that these solutions to my problems require that my perceptions of reality, and my feelings, be aligned more closely with how things truly are (e.g., with the fact that God truly has justified me, and that I am not under law, but grace). So grace and truth must work together, just as Paul and the other apostles knew so well (e.g., see Col. 1:6; John 1:17).

What I find highly interesting is that McLaren teaches us that the issues he and his character Dan Poole (and by extension, myself) have faced are a modern-versus-postmodern matter. That is, postmodernism (as a new way of being a Christian) is *the* way to solve them. But just as in the case of my church, that conclusion is erroneous. We do not need to embrace a postmodern way of being a Christian in order to understand and address such issues. It seems to me that McLaren's own issues, which appear to be remarkably similar to my own, can be explained similarly: namely, that he likely is reacting to his own conservative Christian background and experience.

Does this mean that modernity has *no* influence on the attitudes and traits of Christians that McLaren identifies? No. For example, as Jones has reminded me, it is easy for some pastors to act and preach as though we should never have any doubts about the Bible as our certain foundation.[15] I am not denying that modernity has influenced the ways we have been taught to live as believers. But I *am* denying that McLaren has accurately described modernity, and therefore his solution simply does not follow.

So far I have argued that McLaren and Jones have misdescribed modernity in a key way, and thus they have misidentified the nature of the problems with which they are concerned. In turn, McLaren has misidentified the solution. Here we see that Carson's observation about leaders of the Emerging Church seems right, at least applied to McLaren, for he seems to be reacting to his own conservative Christian background and experience, which was legalistic. But that problem is much too old and much too broad to be explained as merely a "modern" problem. Legalism has existed right from the beginning of the church age; it is something with which Christians have struggled through two millennia. Yet McLaren seems to have concluded that modernity's influence on Christianity is the source of these problems. Thus, McLaren has drawn inappropriate conclusions about the nature of, and solution to, these problems, and he also has inappropriately generalized his conclusions to the church more broadly conceived.

In response, I have suggested (1) that the core issues revolve around clarifying the mistaken notion that we must have certainty in order to have knowledge, and (2) that we need a healthy understanding and appropriation of God's grace and love, held along with truth, to combat the legalistic, rigid, controlling tendencies that McLaren and I have tried to identify. One evangelical leader who is no postmodernist and has written much on grace is Chuck Swindoll, and in considering portions of his *The Grace Awakening Devotional* I am struck by the close relationship and application these points have to many of McLaren's concerns.[16] Swindoll remarks that grace sets us free, making us less concerned about what others think. In a close parallel to McLaren's own concerns, Swindoll observes that as we grow in grace, we will become more tolerant of others, and we will "cultivate a desire for authentic

---

[15] Tony Jones, private e-mail correspondence with me on June 22, 2004.
[16] Charles R. Swindoll, *The Grace Awakening Devotional* (Nashville: W Publishing Group, 2003).

faith rather than endure a religion based on superficial performance."[17] Furthermore, Swindoll identifies the tendency toward legalism all too prevalent in evangelical circles. According to Swindoll, evangelicals tend to give a list of do's and don'ts, as a "legalistic style of strong-arm teaching,"[18] which leaves little or no room for any gray areas. In turn, that leads to a leadership that "maintains strict control over the followers," with a "rigid, self-righteous standard."[19] Swindoll pulls no punches and asserts that "the ranks of Christianity are full of those who compare and would love to control and manipulate you so you will become as miserable as they are."[20] But where grace is freely lived and given, then there can be mercy, something that would allow for real, heart-to-heart sharing of our souls, including our pains and doubts.

If we don't fall into the mistaken trap that we must have certainty to have knowledge (even in our practice, such as in preaching, or in our attitudes); if we practice grace and lovingkindness together with truth; if we provide safe places for people to share their souls deeply and thereby connect with one another; if we provide deeply satisfying theological teaching, which engages the intellect and the whole person; and if we really seek to live out the faith in deeply authentic ways, as Jesus' disciples did; then it does not seem to me that we need to adopt a postmodern way of being a Christian in order to resolve the problems McLaren and Jones see in the church.

We can embrace *both* grace *and* truth, and we can wed truth together with a richly experiential Christian life, full of the experience of God's presence and person. But this has not been a historic strength of evangelicalism. So Dallas Willard is right when he observes that "the sad truth is that you can be an evangelical in excellent standing" without experiences of "our ongoing walk with Jesus Christ and the integrity of soul that permits one to worship the Father in Spirit and truth." He continues:

> Certainly the folks who fit the term post-evangelical are not right about everything, but here they are on to something of extreme impor-

---

[17] Ibid., 22.
[18] Ibid., 44.
[19] Ibid.
[20] Ibid., 69.

tance to anyone concerned about the cause of Christ and the welfare of human beings today.[21]

We need to listen to what postmodern Christians (or, post-evangelicals) are saying in this key regard, too, so that we wed together a life full of rich Christian experience and a life built on truth. And we need carefully to hear their criticisms of contemporary, conservative Christianity. As I have tried to show, they have some important insights we must consider. But we don't need to embrace postmodernism in order to have both experience and knowledge of truth.

And, if we do not embrace postmodernism as a new way of being a Christian, it does not follow that we will end up with a God who has been shrunken to modern tastes, which McLaren says will not appeal to postmodern people.[22] That fear is simply misplaced. I think he has in part misdiagnosed the cause of the problems he addresses, and therefore he has misprescribed the solution.

But there is another key way in which McLaren and Jones have inaccurately described modernity. Stated another way, they have omitted a key aspect of the Enlightenment. That aspect is empiricism, the view that all knowledge comes by way of the five senses. McLaren and Jones have much to say about the Enlightenment overconfidence in human reason (as evidenced in rationalism), but they do not address empiricism, which is at least as important a factor in modernity as rationalism. In so doing, they overlook a key view of Enlightenment thought that finds a contemporary expression in postmodernism: namely, that we are so influenced by something that we cannot know the real world. We are left to construct our own world(s).

THE MISDESCRIPTION OF POSTMODERNITY

This omission or oversight has an extension. McLaren does not explain for his readers that postmodernity involves not just a description of cultural factors but also a normative, philosophical thesis that we are inside language and cannot get "out," to know the real world. Here we can

---

[21] Dallas Willard, foreword to Dave Tomlinson, *The Post-Evangelical*, revised North American edition (Grand Rapids, Mich.: Zondervan/emergentYS, 2003), 12.
[22] Brian McLaren, *More Ready Than You Realize* (Grand Rapids, Mich.: Zondervan, 2002), 52.

see a serious weakness in his two narratives, *A New Kind of Christian* and *The Story We Find Ourselves In*. In these books, Neo asserts that we can stay at the descriptive level of postmodern thought without having to get into all of its philosophical underpinnings. He mentions several authors, such as Derrida, Richard Rorty, Michael Polanyi, and Lesslie Newbigin. Where I think McLaren does his readers a disservice is that he never mentions any concerns with what the constructivist views of such writers imply, or what such views might do to the faith, if we truly recast Christianity itself in a postmodern way of thinking. And, from what we have seen before, McLaren certainly should express such concerns. As a reminder, Derrida thinks there are no identities, so that no two things are identical (even the uses of a word). There always will be *differance* between them, and we are "inside" language. We cannot get at the meaning of an author of a text; instead, our interpretations tell us more about ourselves than about what the author meant. What would that imply for Scripture? It would imply that we cannot know what God meant when He gave us His special revelation, and therefore its meaning is "up to us."

Rorty is also a constructivist, and he has given up on our ability to know the real world (i.e., an extra-linguistic one). He calls that "the world well lost."[23] Here is how he puts it:

> The notion of "the world" as used in a phrase like "different conceptual schemes carve up the world differently" must be the notion of something completely unspecified and unspecifiable—the thing-in-itself, in fact. As soon as we start thinking of "the world" as atoms and the void, or sense data and awareness of them . . . we have changed the name of the game. For we are now well within some particular theory about how the world is.[24]

For Rorty, we simply cannot know the real world; we always work within our theories. What then does that imply for doctrines like Jesus' historical, literal, bodily resurrection? It cannot be a fact of history that we can know, so it ends up being just a construction of our Christian community.

---

[23] Richard Rorty, "The World Well Lost," *The Journal of Philosophy* 69 (October 26, 1972): 649-665.
[24] Ibid., 663.

Polanyi underscores the importance of what he calls "tacit knowledge." Skill is tacit, embodied knowledge. Polanyi argues against the idea that we can have impersonal, exact observations, and instead he collapses facts and values. That is, facts cannot be separated from the values we bring to the data as knowing subjects. To put the idea differently, in philosophy of science, he denies a distinction between discoveries and their justification, or supporting evidence, so that what supports a belief and the "facts" that have been "discovered" are not somehow independent of each other.[25] Rather, "discoveries" and "facts" are what they are in light of a "fiduciary" framework of beliefs and values (i.e., a set of beliefs held by a faith commitment) that people bring to the data.

Newbigin, according to Kevin Vanhoozer, thinks the "postmodern critique of foundationalism has shown that human thinking always takes place within 'fiduciary' frameworks" of belief.[26] Newbigin explicitly draws on Polanyi, who says "we must now recognize belief once more as the source of all knowledge. . . . No intelligence, however critical or original, can operate outside such a fiduciary framework."[27] Newbigin extends Polanyi by claiming that "no 'fiduciary framework' or 'pattern' . . . can exist except as it is held by a community."[28] In these quotes, we see, first, that for Newbigin and Polanyi *belief* becomes an essential *source* of knowledge, a view with which I will disagree in chapter 9. I will argue, instead, that we can have direct access to objects in the real world and be aware of them as they are, and that we may then form beliefs about them. Second, both Newbigin and Polanyi hold that we must work within frameworks of belief, but I will disagree again in chapter 9 for the same reasons. Third, Newbigin ties such frameworks to communities, a move that is similar to what Kallenberg and others have done. These comments do not necessarily mean that Newbigin or

---

[25] For example, see the discussion by R. T. Allen, "Polanyi, Michael," in *Routledge Encyclopedia of Philosophy*, ed. E. Craig, retrieved July 23, 2004, from http://www.rep.routledge.com/article/DD079SECT3.

[26] Kevin J. Vanhoozer, "Pilgrim's Digress: How to Think Christianly on the Way About the Way," in *Christianity and the Postmodern Turn*, ed. Myron Penner (Grand Rapids, Mich.: Brazos, 2005).

[27] Michael Polanyi, *Personal Knowledge*, 267, cited in J. E. Lesslie Newbigin, "The Other Side of 1984: Questions for the Churches," in *Risk No. 18* (Geneva: World Council of Churches, 1983), 17, accessed from www.newbigin.net/assets/pdf/83os84.pdf on August 26, 2004. [Note: Although it is not indicated in Newbigin's reference, Polanyi's book has been published by Harper & Row, 1964.]

[28] Newbigin, "The Other Side of 1984," 18.

Polanyi thinks we are trapped "behind" something and cannot ever have cognitive contact with an objective reality, but that ability has been attenuated, by their assessment, to say the least.

So there are ample reasons in these thinkers, as well as in others whom McLaren cites approvingly (such as Murphy, Grenz, and Franke), to see significant constructivist elements. As we already have seen, the linguistic constructivist thought of people such as Kallenberg, Hauerwas, Grenz, and Franke has several serious flaws. Though McLaren himself is not a philosopher by training, his characters make several assertions that also seem to indicate a strong propensity toward constructivist thought.

McLaren tells us that there is "nothing purely 'objective'" in God's creation, meaning that all has personal value.[29] Here, he uses "objective" in the sense that there is nothing purely neutral and disinterested, and not necessarily in the sense that there are some things that exist in their own right, whether or not we talk or think about them, see them, etc. Elsewhere he seems to indicate, much like Hauerwas and Kallenberg, that we cannot achieve an objective vantage point, in that our viewpoints are limited, contingent, changing, and not privileged.[30] He seems to be suggesting that we cannot achieve a neutral position from which we can know truth, so that we cannot stand outside our particular, historically located position and know objective, universal truths.

Furthermore, McLaren tells us that to "understand anything, we need to apprentice ourselves to the community that honors what it is we want to understand."[31] It seems he is criticizing the idea that truths are abstractions that are knowable in principle to anyone, regardless of standpoint. This seems quite close to what Kallenberg and Hauerwas mean when they claim that meaning is a matter of language use within a community, for there are no ahistorical, freestanding truths we may know apart from communities which have constructed their worlds by their particular languages.

In light of this claim, let us consider a couple of cases. Consider first a solitary person who has been stranded on an island. Suppose further

---

[29] McLaren, *More Ready Than You Realize*, 94.
[30] Ibid., 76.
[31] Ibid., 77.

that this is a very young child, who knows nothing about science or logic. There is no community present to check up on his or her use of terms, so it is possible the child could misuse his or her terms and not be aware of it. Could this person gain an understanding of some of the laws of nature, or laws of logic, without being in a community?

It surely seems the child could gain such understanding, just by observing the world and how things function. For instance, the child could infer the law of gravity by observing that things always fall down to the earth when unattached to things to hold them up. Or, he or she could observe that a set of five stones is larger (has more members) than a set of three stones, which in turn is larger than a set of two stones. Does this child have to be apprenticed to a community to understand these concepts? Surely not.

Therefore it is at least the case that McLaren has overstated his view. But he could still claim that most of reality is a construction. As I read postmodern philosophers and theologians, they might hold varying views as to the extent of the constructivist enterprise. Some people, such as Grenz and Franke, seem to leave some room for truths that exist apart from our language use in community, such as in regards to the existence of the material world.[32] Jean Porter seems to hold a similar position in regards to the "fact" of evolution.[33] On the other hand, while Kallenberg thinks there is a real world, he is so concerned about "bifurcating" world and language that it seems hard for him to even conceive of a language-independent reality. So McLaren could reply that, yes, natural laws and laws of logic are not constructions, but that still leaves much room for him to hold that most of "reality" is a construction. Yet, he also informs us through his characters that "all is contextual," that "no meanings can exist without context."[34] So, it seems that he is taking a firm stance on the nature of truth—that we know it from the standpoint of being located within a community that has been formed by that community's language.

What else may we see in regards to McLaren's own beliefs on the social construction of reality? McLaren's character Neo says that history

---

[32] Stanley J. Grenz and John R. Franke, *Beyond Foundationalism* (Knoxville: Westminster/John Knox Press, 2001), 53.
[33] Jean Porter, *Natural and Divine Law* (Grand Rapids, Mich.: Eerdmans, 1999), 102.
[34] Brian McLaren, *A New Kind of Christian* (San Francisco: Jossey-Bass, 2001), 106.

began with our ability to write it.[35] That is a remarkable statement; how should we understand it? Taken at face value, it seems that he equates history itself with the writing of it. That is, the writing of history makes it what it is. This interpretation is closely aligned with what Kallenberg and others have told us. However, surely there were human (and non-human) events that took place before anyone wrote about them. But McLaren at least implies that that is not the case—that is, our telling the story constructs and makes the events what they are.

Elsewhere, McLaren tells us through Neo that a huge part of us flows from language, but he does not explain or qualify this statement, so we are left in a position to speculate just what this might mean. If he means that we express our self-understanding in language, that surely is the case. But if we have enough other reasons to think that he believes, like Kallenberg and our other authors, that we are "inside" language and cannot get "out," then that clarifies what he means here: we are what we are in light of how we (as individuals, together with other members of our community) tell our stories. If there is no existence we know of apart from language use, then we too are made what we are by our use of language.

Further along in *A New Kind of Christian,* McLaren through Neo asserts that though we live on the same planet, "we live in different universes—depending on the kind of God we believe in and on our understanding of the master story we are a part of."[36] This is a fascinating statement. In ordinary experience, it may sometimes seem as though we live in different worlds, in that some may have such radically different ways of seeing the *same* world (e.g., from a Christian perspective versus an atheistic or Buddhist perspective). But in light of McLaren's other comments, as well as his appeal to many postmodern authors who support a form of constructivism, it seems that he thinks we live in a linguistic world of our own making, even though, like Grenz and Franke, he believes there is something to the existence of the physical universe that is real apart from the human constructive task. This seems to be what he means, and if not, then he needs to clarify himself.

But what of Jones? I argued in chapter 3 that he too accepts the

---

[35] Ibid., 14.
[36] Ibid., 161.

internal relation of language and world, and so his views too will end up being that the world is a construction made by our language use. Yet, couldn't he reply that I have overlooked his key point, namely, that we all have our subjective viewpoints and biases? After all, he points out that we as believers love the Bible and are not neutral about it, so how can we be objective? I think we can reply by making a couple of distinctions. For one, certainly Jones is right in saying that we all have our particularity, interests, cultural and emotional baggage, desires, and loves. It is true that these things can cloud our judgments, interpretations, and theorizing. But those are different issues than the main one I have been stressing, namely, can we know how things really are in the objectively existing world? We still can be influenced and conditioned by our culture, etc., and yet know objective truth (e.g., that 2+2=4, that murder is wrong). And, in chapter 9, I will try to explain more fully that we do know such truths, and to show how that happens.

It seems to be the case that McLaren believes we live in a linguistic world of our own making, since we are "inside" language and cannot get "outside" it. If so, then McLaren faces a set of challenges that his view must answer. Through Neo, McLaren tells us that as those who are pioneering a new, postmodern way of being Christians, "we need to engage the best thinking," to examine this approach in light of biblical, theological, philosophical, and other insights.[37] As I see it, some crucial challenges he faces are these: he needs to solve the problems I posed in the preceding chapter regarding the postmodern, constructivist views. He also needs to address issues I raised in this chapter. In the next chapter, I will pose more direct challenges, ones that stem from what a "postmodernization" of the faith will do to orthodox Christianity. To those implications and effects we now turn.

---

[37] Brian McLaren, *The Story We Find Ourselves In* (San Francisco: Jossey-Bass, 2003), 164.

*"Furthermore, one might even suppose,
from a commonly held theistic [i.e., Christian]
point of view, that if God wants to he can
communicate with human beings, bring them to know,
how things really are apart from their descriptions.
All of this remains impossible, however,
on the received [epistemological] view. . . . God can't
get out and we can't get out, and if God could get out
he could never tell us how things are apart
from our concepts/language. We are left to 'construct'
him and what he says, along with everything else,
from within our 'circle of ideas' or our language."*

DALLAS WILLARD
**"HOW CONCEPTS RELATE THE MIND TO ITS OBJECTS:
THE 'GOD'S EYE VIEW' VINDICATED?" 20**

SEVEN

ASSESSING POSTMODERNISM'S EFFECT ON CHRISTIAN BELIEFS AND MINISTRY

Not only are there many issues with postmodernism in general, many other issues arise when Christians apply its ideas to their faith. The crucial question will be this: can Christianity survive a transformation into a linguistic approach, as advocated by Hauerwas, Kallenberg, Grenz, Franke, Murphy, and Jones? Theologically, I will argue that it cannot; there are certain core doctrines that simply will be compromised by such a move. We also will see the implications of postmodernism for Christian ethics, when we look at the doctrine of sanctification. Finally, one of the supposed strengths of postmodernism (authenticity) will actually turn out to be a severe weakness, for with postmodernism we will lose the real Jesus.

But why should these kinds of conclusions follow? After all, aren't the people whose work we are reviewing evangelical writers who love the Lord, who believe that salvation is through Christ alone? That is, they seem to be holding to key orthodox positions, despite some of their innovations, such as their linguistic emphases. I propose, however, to show that their views are inconsistent with orthodoxy, by trying to take their views more seriously and consistently than I have seen them do.

GOD AND SPECIAL REVELATION

We saw in chapter 5 that Grenz and Franke hold that while we are on the "inside" of language, the Holy Spirit can and does speak to the many local churches today, and presumably this is how God was able to give us special revelation in the Scriptures. That is, while we are on the "inside" of language, God is not so limited, and thus Christians still can know objective truth as God has revealed it in Scripture. This is a natural, attractive answer to the charge that since we are on the "inside" of language, we cannot know objective truth, even though we think God has revealed it in the Bible.

As natural as this response may seem, however, it is mistaken. The important issue is not that God can break through, or even whether He is participating in our language games. Rather, it is that we are on the "inside" of language and its influences and cannot get "outside" of it to know reality. Special revelation is an aspect of reality. Accordingly, on this postmodern view, we cannot know such truth for what it is. Nor can we know the meaning that the biblical authors had in mind, for meaning is primarily how the text is used within a specific community, and we live in different ones now than those that existed at the time when Scripture was being revealed. For example, the group of Christians Paul taught at Ephesus is not the exact same community as the one I fellowship with at Trinity Evangelical Free Church in Redlands, California. But, according to postmodernism, even though we cannot know the intended meaning the authors had in mind, we can make the text into what it is for us by how we use it within our communities. Hence, there is an inescapably constructive work that we as Christians do when we read and use the Scriptures. We make it into what it is by how we use it within our local communities!

So the prospects for divine revelation seem dismal at best, if not outright impossible. And what implications does this view have for God Himself? Historically, orthodox Christians have believed that God makes Himself known through the Bible and in the person of Jesus, and that God's being and character are independent of our talk or beliefs about Him. By the postmodern view, however, we cannot know reality as it truly (i.e., objectively) is. So, we cannot know God as He is, either. Thus, we may say nothing about God unless such talk has been made part of the rules of our community's language games. By Kallenberg's view, as well as that of Grenz, Franke, and Hauerwas, since we are on the "inside" of language and thus cannot know God as He really is (for He too exists objectively), Christians must *make* God.

What do I mean by this? Quite simply, Christians cannot know God as He is if we are on the "inside" of the pervasive influences of language, as these Christian postmodernists believe. Just like any other aspect of our "reality," Christians construct God by how they talk. We make God into what He is—for us. This conclusion, however, results in the absurd condition that Christians *must* be idolaters. In this case, we do not make God in our own image, or out of wood or stone, but nevertheless we make God by how we talk. But this result contradicts Scripture, which clearly commands us not to make any likeness of God, or any idols. Therefore, two conclusions follow: (1) Even if our Christian postmodern authors' view happens to be right—that we are "inside" language— the logical result of that condition is that Christians end up contradicting their own "grammar," that is, the Scriptures, and so we cannot hope to live according to what the Bible teaches. But we already have seen ample reasons not to believe that we are "inside" language. In that case, another conclusion follows: (2) Christians dare not embrace this view, for it necessitates that we be idolaters, something that surely will undermine Christianity.

But as serious as these conclusions may be, there are other severe problems with the "linguistic method" of these postmoderns when applied to Christianity. Let us turn to examine other such issues.

JESUS: HIS INCARNATION, RESURRECTION, AND ATONEMENT

Historically, orthodox Christians have maintained that Jesus is God, who took on human nature in the Incarnation. Hence, He is perfect God and perfect man; He has two natures. As such, Jesus seems to be the ideal person to communicate special revelation, since He would know both human and divine languages, so that He could communicate God's truth in human language. It seems that Hauerwas, Kallenberg, Grenz, and Franke could argue that it is in the person of Jesus that God has successfully given us objective truth, even though we cannot get "outside" of language. God has solved the dilemma and revealed such truth, or so they might argue.

Again, this is a natural answer, but it too has its problems. Consider Jesus' divine nature. It would seem that, since Jesus is God, He would not have the sort of limitations that we as humans have. As God, Jesus would not be "stuck" on the "inside" of language as we humans are. But what about Jesus as a human being? If humans are on the "inside" of language, it is a reasonable expectation that as a man, Jesus, too, would be "inside" language. Accordingly, we are faced with a fully divine person who is able to get "outside" of language but who, as also a fully human being, cannot escape language. And even worse, He experiences *both* situations at the same time! This dilemma would be unlivable and would suggest that Jesus would be radically schizophrenic. Moreover, God would be foolish to even attempt the Incarnation, knowing that it could not achieve its intended result of revealing objective truths.

Let us consider another issue regarding Jesus' life. Historically, orthodox Christians have affirmed that the crucifixion and resurrection were events that took place in history. That is, they were objective events that actually happened, and we can know them to be real events. Such Christians have understood the crucifixion to be the event in which Jesus *actually* bore the sins of all people and paid for them in full, regardless of how people describe this event in language. Peter puts it this way: "Christ died for sins once for all, the righteous for the unrighteous, to bring you to God. He was put to death in the body but made alive by the Spirit" (1 Pet. 3:18, NIV). Likewise, Paul underscores the historicity of the resurrection by the claims he makes in 1 Corinthians 15:

> For what I received I passed on to you as of first importance: that Christ died for our sins according to the Scriptures, that he was buried, that he was raised on the third day according to the Scriptures, and that he appeared to Peter, and then to the Twelve. . . .
>
> But if it is preached that Christ has been raised from the dead, how can some of you say that there is no resurrection of the dead? If there is no resurrection of the dead, then not even Christ has been raised. And if Christ has not been raised, our preaching is useless and so is your faith. More than that, we are then found to be false witnesses about God, for we have testified about God that he raised Christ from the dead. But he did not raise him if in fact the dead are not raised. For if the dead are not raised, then Christ has not been raised either. And if Christ has not been raised, your faith is futile (1 Cor. 15:3-5, 12-17, NIV).

Such beliefs in the historicity of the crucifixion and resurrection make no sense on a view where we cannot know objective truths, and where we make our truths by how we talk. It seems that according to Hauerwas, Kallenberg, Grenz, and Franke's view, Christians make these events into what they are (for them) by how they talk about them. We cannot know these events as they actually were; such knowledge would be impossible, according to their Christian postmodernist view.

Notice what happens to these core Christian doctrines if we adopt their Christian postmodernist view. Consider first the resurrection. If there is no objective, language-independent world we can know, then Christians must make their world, which includes their view that Jesus died and rose from the dead. Therefore, for Christians to claim that Jesus *really* rose from the dead is equivalent to the statement that Christians *say* that Jesus rose from the dead.

But we should see that this understanding simply changes the meaning of the resurrection as an event that objectively happened in history. To help get a handle on this, imagine that we are at a funeral and we are standing before the open casket. Here, we face a grim reality: this person is dead. We may use various words to describe the person, such as "dead," "deceased," "departed," or "he [or she] is with the Lord," and such words help us grasp the reality of the situation. Regardless of which words are spoken, there remains a fact of the matter—the person is dead, and that reality will not change no matter which words we use to describe the situation. The body's organs will not suddenly function, the person awaken and then arise out of the coffin. Language simply does not have that power.

Let us apply this insight to the resurrection of Jesus. Jesus' resurrection simply cannot be due to Christians' language use. No *mere* human person (or group of people) has that kind of power, to make a dead person rise. Of course, Jesus spoke and commanded dead people, such as Lazarus, to return to life (see John 11:38ff.), as did His apostles (e.g., Acts 9:36-41, and 20:9-10). He spoke as One with the authority and power to change such a state. But for the rest of us, constructing the world in such a way that Jesus rose from the dead simply is *not* a power of language. We all know that language does not have that kind of power, and even in Jesus' case, He brought the dead back to life by the exercise of His authority and power and not just by His happening to speak certain words. Christians could never make Jesus rise from the dead by their use of language. But that means that Hauerwas, Kallenberg, Grenz, and Franke's view cannot make sense of the resurrection, or preserve its status as an objective, historical event.

Second, what happens to the atonement in their Christian postmodernist view? In similar fashion, the atonement Jesus made for our sins ends up not being an objective reality that we can know occurred when He died on the cross. To be consistent according to the linguistic method of Hauerwas, Kallenberg, Grenz, and Franke, the status of the atoning sacrifice of Jesus must be dependent upon the way Christians talk. By their view, Christians make the truth conditions for their own forgiveness by how they talk. They talk in such a way that they create a world in which sin and forgiveness are real issues. But that will not be the case for other worlds, which have been made by others (e.g., secularists, or Muslims).

However, forgiveness of sins does not seem to be a power of language, or at least of human language. As the writer of Hebrews puts it, "without the shedding of blood there is no forgiveness" (Heb. 9:22, NIV). Peter also clearly states, "Christ died for sins once for all, the righteous for the unrighteous, to bring you to God. He was put to death in the body but made alive by the Spirit" (1 Pet. 3:18, NIV). These verses emphasize that the atonement took place as an objective, historical event, one that we can know as such. But if these conditions are made true merely by how Christians talk, then Christians would create by how they talk the truthfulness of their claims. But it seems clear that we have no such power to create these "facts" by our language use.

These problems arise when Christian doctrines are thought to *be* linguistic constructions. Instead, it seems essential for orthodox Christianity that these events should be understood as being objective, language-independent truths. Now we will shift to examine the implications of Christian postmodernists' views for the doctrines of justification and sanctification.

JUSTIFICATION

The Reformer John Calvin explained justification in this way: "We simply interpret justification, as the acceptance with which God receives us into his favour as if we were righteous; and we say that this justification consists in the forgiveness of sins and the imputation of the righteousness of Christ."[1] As with the meaning of any other concept, however, the views of Hauerwas, Kallenberg, Grenz, and Franke would require that justification be defined in terms of language and behavior. "Appropriate" behaviors demonstrate that a person is justified before God.

How might this look? Such behaviors might include the participation in the taking of communion, or attending Bible studies. Additional behaviors likely would include telling the gospel to others and saying things like "I received Jesus as my Savior when I was ten years old." Also, people might sing along in church with praise music, even lifting up their hands, as to the Lord.

But does it follow that, if someone exhibits these or other such behaviors, he or she is justified before God? Suppose the person says, "I received Jesus as my Lord and Savior when I was ten years old." This expression *seems* clearly to indicate that the person is saved and therefore justified. Even so, it is *possible* that the individual said these words in order to be accepted by others in a Christian group. Or, maybe by saying this, the person would be allowed to enter the group and thereby get a free meal. Or perhaps the person might have believed that by saying this, the Christian group would accept him or her, and that would cause the individual's desired termination from teaching in the natural sciences at a nearby college. The possibilities, even though they may seem far-fetched, are virtually endless.

What these possibilities should tell us is, first, that behavior, without reference to what the person intended, is ambiguous. Any given behavior could be explained by any number of possible intentions in the mind of the one doing the actions. Second, we also should learn that what a person means by his or her actions always depends on that individual's intentions. Behavior may be a good indication of what someone meant, but meaning is not primarily a matter of behavior, contrary to what Hauerwas and Kallenberg have told us. Much more fundamentally, meaning is a matter of what someone had in mind (i.e., his or her intentions) when that person did some action.

---

[1] John Calvin, *Institutes of the Christian Religion*, trans. Henry Beveridge, book 3, chapter 11 (Grand Rapids, Mich.: Eerdmans, 1997), 38.

So behaviors that typically indicate that a person is justified are no guarantee that someone really is justified before God. To put it differently, these kinds of behaviors are not sufficient for someone to be justified. But are such behaviors even required, or necessary, to be justified? While we should expect certain kinds of behaviors of a real, regenerated believer, orthodox Christians have held that such behaviors in public are not necessary for justification. Consider the example of Nicodemus as well as Joseph of Arimathea, who were secret followers of Jesus even before they took a public stand by requesting the body of Jesus for burial. Being secret believers, they would have been quite careful not to give away their real belief by how they spoke or acted in public. Even so, they were followers of Jesus, and later they did indeed show their loyalty to Him.

There is another ironic result of this postmodern view, when we test it for consistency. Why is reconciliation with God the greatest need of humanity? Why are we sinners, and in need of Christ's redemption? If this Christian postmodern view is right, it is because that is how Christians talk and make their world. It cannot be because that is our *real*, objective condition, for by this view, we cannot know any such things!

Furthermore, justification is a process, by this view, as Jones tells us.[2] It is not a once-for-all act that occurs when a person puts his or her trust in Christ as Savior. Rather, it is a process of adopting the Christian way of life as one's primary communal affiliation and identification. That process requires learning the language (and thus the verbal and nonverbal behaviors) as an insider of the Christian community, and it takes time and effort to cultivate skill and fluency in Christian language and behavior. But Scripture teaches explicitly that justification is an action that takes place at a point in time (the significance of the aorist tense in Greek). In Romans 5:1, Paul declares that, "having been justified by faith, we have peace with God through our Lord Jesus Christ." That is, at a point in time, when we trusted in Christ, we were justified, so justification is not a process. Compare Hebrews 10:14: "For by one offering He has perfected for all time those who are sanctified" (or, "are being sanctified," NASB margin). In Christ, God has perfected us (perfect tense); the effect was brought about at a point in time and the results go

---

[2] Tony Jones, *Postmodern Youth Ministry* (Grand Rapids, Mich.: Zondervan/Youth Specialties, 2001), 133.

on forever. But that orthodox view is mistaken, according to the Christian postmodern view. For Hauerwas, conversion is not really a choice at all; rather, it is "a long process of being baptismally engrafted into a new people, an alternative *polis,* a countercultural social structure called church."[3]

We turn now to the doctrine of sanctification.

SANCTIFICATION, ETHICS, AND IMPLICATIONS FOR CHRISTIAN WITNESS

While justification does not seem to be transmutable into a linguistic approach, perhaps the doctrine of sanctification could be explained well by Hauerwas, Kallenberg, Grenz, Franke, McLaren and Jones's account. Why might this be the case? Sanctification emphasizes the process of becoming like Jesus in our character, and that process *should* result in certain kinds of behaviors. Ethically speaking, this is a Christian version of what is called virtue ethics, which places its focus not so much on principles to obey (although it has room for them), but rather on character. So, though our authors' emphasis on language and behavior fails in relation to other core doctrines, perhaps it may succeed in this one.

Let us make a couple of observations about the impact of these writers' views on the doctrine of sanctification. For one, by their view, a believer's character qualities, or virtues, as well as his or her standing before God, are constructions of how Christians use their language. They are not objective qualities of a real world that we can know. Again, Christians create the very conditions they say are so important, and then they fulfill them by how they talk.

Second, Hauerwas and Kallenberg stress a critical aspect of living out the character qualities of Jesus, that of being a witness to non-Christians by how we live. By their view, we cannot just go out and "say" the truth of the gospel to "outsiders." That is because the meaning of our words derives from their use within the Christian community, and therefore we cannot just tell non-Christians how and why we believe. We literally speak different languages. Accordingly, we should not witness to them simply by reading a tract (which, following McLaren, tends to reduce the gospel to simple steps), or by giving typical apologetical arguments, such

---

[3] Stanley Hauerwas and William H. Willimon, *Resident Aliens* (Nashville: Abingdon, 1989), 46.

as for Jesus' resurrection, or for the beginning of the universe. All these kinds of arguments and approaches are mistaken, they would say, because we speak different languages, and those traditional apologetical approaches all presuppose that we can step outside of language and know how things really are (e.g., that we can know the objective facts of history that prove that Jesus rose from the dead).

Let us examine this issue of witnessing more closely. Surely, as Christians, Hauerwas, Kallenberg, Grenz, and Franke would want to preserve the crucial Christian "practice" of witnessing. For them, we do not witness by just talking to non-Christians; we witness to those outside of our Christian community by *showing* them the truthfulness of our story by how we live. Thus, witnessing is closely related to ethics in that our character is crucial for witnessing. Again, as we should expect, the emphasis is on our behavior. Hauerwas explains that the church is a community

> . . . in which people are faithful to their promises, love their enemies, tell the truth, honor the poor, suffer for righteousness, and thereby testify to the amazing community-creating power of God. . . . this church [the confessing one] knows that its most credible form of witness (and the most "effective" thing it can do for the world) is the actual creation of a living, breathing, visible community of faith.[4]

And, as Jesus says, all people will know that Christians are His disciples if they love one another.

But on the basis of these authors' linguistic, postmodern approach, how should we understand their claim that we witness by showing others the truthfulness of our story? Due to their view that we should not separate world and language, it must be a claim that has been made from within their Christian communities. As such, it is a sweeping, universal claim, and its truthfulness is due to the fact that this is how their particular communities talk. But which local Christian communities are these? It cannot be some generalized Christian community, since those authors emphasize the discrete, particular character of all languages. Yet, they argue as though this is the claim of some generalized Christian community.

---

[4] Ibid., 46-47 (bracketed insert mine).

But as we have seen before, they do not specify in enough detail what are the specific communities out of which they write. If we take their view seriously and consistently, then it is critical that we know the precise identity of these local communities, because we may not share the specific commitments and understandings and the specific language of those communities. But couldn't they reply that the Scriptures themselves unify the various discrete Christian communities? We have seen this kind of move before, where Grenz and Franke appeal to the Holy Spirit to do this unifying work. But this move will not solve the problem. If meaning is mainly usage, then how the various Christian communities use the Scriptures makes all the difference.

Furthermore, we should observe that the so-called "outsiders" have been made into what they are by these Christians' use of their language in their communities. "Outsiders" can see the truth of the gospel simply because that is how these Christians have talked about and shaped those other people into "outsiders." So this claim that outsiders can see the truthfulness of Christian behaviors is question begging and it has no basis in reality (at least that we can know), based on this postmodern view.

But there are other kinds of problems with Hauerwas, Kallenberg, Grenz, and Franke's view. Muslims also value honesty and care for each other in community. The Christian way of living out these qualities that Hauerwas thinks are so clear in their witness may not be the only way to do so. For instance, different kinds of people honor the poor. Also, non-Christians may conceive of certain qualities in different ways than Christians do. For instance, for Jehovah's Witnesses, suffering for righteousness may not look the same as in a Protestant Christian setting. Jehovah's Witnesses may consider criticism from a Christian while engaged in witnessing to be suffering for righteousness. From a Christian standpoint, however, they have not suffered for the truth. As a different example, a Christian missionary may suffer for righteousness by being martyred for preaching the gospel. But if each community makes its own world by how it talks, there is no way for outsiders to distinguish between alternative behaviors and their meaningfulness in different communities.

So it is not true that these virtuous behaviors are limited to just the Christian community. They also do not have to be performed in the exact same way as Christians would perform them. Thus, according to these authors' view, these behaviors are *ambiguous* to outsiders. Somehow, their witness to the unique truth of Christianity assumes a further standard, one that apparently is so apart from how we talk.

Therefore, this postmodernist view cannot make sense of the importance and effectiveness of Christian witness. Even so, when Christians do live out their faith consistently, it *is* powerful in its witness. Furthermore, from my experience and that of my colleagues and students, apologetical arguments are far from being an outmoded way of communicating the truth of the gospel. How can this be so? I believe that it is due to the fact that Christianity is objectively true, and we can know it to be just that.

THE AUTHENTIC JESUS

Let me make one more observation before we leave our present chapter's discussion. The effectiveness of Christian witness through embodying the faith (the preferred method of Christian postmoderns) hinges on our being able to show to outsiders the authentic Jesus, both in and among us. But *can* a linguistically made community give us the authentic Jesus? I do not see how this is possible, for on this view, as I have repeatedly tried to show, we cannot know objective reality. Therefore, when we press this postmodern view for consistency, all we can end up with in our witness and the Christian life is our *construction* of Jesus. If we claim that we have the authentic Jesus living in our midst, we simply cannot deliver on what postmoderns value, namely, authenticity! Furthermore, knowingly appealing to authenticity while at the same time knowing that we can only offer our own linguistically constructed Savior, is the height of hypocrisy. But, we *do* know Jesus, and He is working in our midst today. To explain that requires that we can know reality, at least in part, as it really is, which undermines the core postmodern contention.

WHERE DO WE GO FROM HERE?

Postmodernism, and in particular the Christian postmodernism advocated by the authors we have studied, undercuts objective truth, and it is seriously flawed and mistaken. Not only does it not make sense on philosophical grounds, it also does not make sense when applied to

Christianity. More seriously, it will lead to the demise of Christianity. The faith cannot survive a transformation into being a linguistic construction of how Christians talk.

Having seen how the postmodernist view fails, the question remains: Can we know objective truths? I believe we can and often do know many objective truths, but before I make a positive case for how we can (and often do) know objective truth, we need to return to where we started, by examining the issue of relativism. Is this postmodern approach to the faith relativistic, and if so, is that a serious problem? Here we will address head-on the attraction of many believers to relativism. Having done that, we will be in a position to develop further the case for knowing objective truth.

"For to deny the existence of universally objective moral distinctions, one must admit that Mother Teresa was no more or less moral than Adolf Hitler, that torturing three-year-olds for fun is neither good nor evil, that giving 10 percent of one's financial surplus to an invalid is neither praiseworthy nor condemnable, that raping a woman is neither right nor wrong, and that providing food and shelter for one's spouse and children is neither a good thing nor a bad thing."

FRANCIS J. BECKWITH AND GREGORY KOUKL
RELATIVISM: FEET FIRMLY PLANTED IN MID-AIR, 13

EIGHT

ADDRESSING THE CHALLENGE OF RELATIVISM

In my critique of postmodernism, I deliberately have left for last the question of relativism. When Hauerwas, Kallenberg, Grenz, and Franke argue that there is no essence to language, but there are only many languages, and each community makes its world by how its members talk, it seems at first glance that their views are, quite simply, relativistic. Many people therefore draw the further conclusion that, being relativistic, their views should be rejected.[1] Yet I think too many people make serious mistakes by leading off with the charge that the views of these Christian postmoderns are relativistic. As we will see, they have ways to rebut that charge, and if that is all we can say about the matter, then maybe they will have succeeded in showing that their views are not relativistic. After we examine their replies, we will return to the challenge of relativism more broadly conceived. Though many Christians today think ethics, for instance, is relative, should we as Christians believe that?

REBUTTING THE CHARGE OF RELATIVISM

First, Kallenberg has offered a very sophisticated answer to the charge that his views are just another kind of relativism.[2] Basically, he argues that relativism presumes we can know universal truth from an objective

---

[1] For further reading, see my discussion in *Virtue Ethics and Moral Knowledge: Philosophy of Language After MacIntyre and Hauerwas* (Aldershot, England: Ashgate, 2003), chapter 8.

[2] See Brad J. Kallenberg, *Ethics as Grammar: Changing the Postmodern Subject* (Notre Dame, Ind.: University of Notre Dame Press, 2001), 227-250. I also discuss his "solution" in my "Conceptual Problems for Stanley Hauerwas's Virtue Ethics," *Philosophia Christi* 3:1 (2001): 160-164.

standpoint. That is, the charge of relativism is based on a mistaken notion that we can somehow get outside of language and see that one view *really* is relative when compared to an objective standard. But he quickly reminds us that this view is impossible! We always are working from the "inside" of language, he says, so even the charge that his views are relativistic are just those uttered from within some particular community (and one whose members still think—mistakenly, on Kallenberg's view—that they can know objective truth). For Kallenberg, relativism ends up being a nonissue.

Let us consider two lines of response to this claim. First, we already have seen that Kallenberg as well as Hauerwas, Grenz, and Franke most likely presuppose that they too have access to objective truth. For instance, either (1) their very claim that language and world are internally related is a claim made according to how they talk in their respective communities, and how they have constructed their worlds (but if that is all that this claim amounts to, then why should anyone outside their communities talk as they do?); or, as is far more likely, (2) this claim actually betrays a significant presupposition—that they actually presuppose they can know reality as it truly is, apart from language, in order to deny that that access is possible. If that is the case, then Kallenberg's seemingly effective rebuttal of the charge of relativism is not successful after all.

Or, on my second, alternate interpretation, all his reply amounts to is just a way his particular, local Christian community happens to talk. However, he never tells us which particular Christian community it is out of which he writes, so we do not have enough information, even on his own postmodern views, to know if we would want to identify ourselves with that community. By way of reminder, it makes all the difference which community is his, since, by his view, there is no essence to Christian language, but only localized Christian languages. The fact that he has not detailed that community enables him to make sweeping claims that supposedly are normative for all Christians. But all that claim amounts to, at least on my second interpretation, is just the way his particular community's members happen to talk. If that is the case, then *so what* if that is how they talk? But he does not write in a way as to indicate that all he wants to do is say that this is how his local community happens to talk. No, he writes in a general way so as to get other Christians to think in the same way as he does. Therefore, it seems much more likely that he does presuppose a way "out" of language, in order to deny that such access (or, that the ability to have such access) is possible. So, his rebuttal to the charge of relativism ends up being ineffective.

As a second kind of attempt to rebut the charge of relativism, Hauerwas, Kallenberg, Grenz, and Franke could reply that what makes their view not relativistic is that they write as Christians, who have the revealed, objective truth from God. Even though we are on the inside of language, it still is okay to make such a claim because God has given us the objective truth. Now, it is true that God has given us objective truth in the Scriptures. But their appeal to this view fails, too, for as we discussed before, by their view we still must interpret (and therefore construct) revelation by the particular rules of our community.

What should we make, then, of the charge that Christian postmodernists espouse relativism? For one, despite their claims to the contrary, their views do not escape from being relativistic. Additionally, the ways in which that gets particularly troublesome is that it makes the gospel just one among many religious stories, without a viable way to know that we have the actual (i.e., objectively true) message of salvation.[3] It also allows for even the most horrendous acts to be justified by people who simply align themselves with a community that accepts those acts. What bin Laden and his fellow terrorists did on September 11, 2001, was morally praiseworthy according to them, but not according to Christians, nor for most other people. By this postmodern view, there is nothing left for Christians to do but to simply say that we do not believe in such things, and then live our lives in such a way as to model how Jesus would have treated people. But all that means is that this is how Christians talk and live, without a defensible way to adjudicate between what bin Laden would say and what Christians would say. There does not seem to be a moral basis for deciding between these viewpoints, except to resort to the exercise of power and simply try to enforce some viewpoint.

This is exactly like what would happen on secular campuses if a stu-

---

[3] See my *Virtue Ethics and Moral Knowledge*, 106–108, and 136–137, for a discussion of how Alasdair MacIntyre's widely heralded attempt fails to show the rational superiority of one community (or, in his focus, one "tradition") over another. Furthermore, while I assume here that we can know reality, I will defend that assumption in chapter 9.

dent group did not play by the university administration's rules. There would be no moral basis for enforcing one moral viewpoint over another; it simply would be a resort to power. In the case of bin Laden and other terrorists, we could say that those acts were evil, along with those of Hitler, Stalin, Mao, and others, but if there is no objective moral standard by appeal to which we can decide which views are right and which are wrong, then we are left with an utterly relativistic situation and no moral basis to punish those who commit such acts.

So far, we have addressed problems with Christian postmodern views being relativistic. But perhaps we should ask at this point, *"So what* if their views are relativistic?" After all, from what we have seen, many believers have accepted the belief that morals are relative. In light of this, we should address two issues. First, why are Christians so willing to believe in ethical relativism? Second, is relativism problematic, in its own right, and especially for Christians? I will answer these two questions in turn.

WHY ARE CHRISTIANS SO WILLING TO EMBRACE ETHICAL RELATIVISM?

There are at least two reasons why believers are tending to embrace relativism. One, for at least a full generation our children have been taught that they must be tolerant of differing viewpoints and people, and that all viewpoints are equally valid. The broader culture has inculcated this view, and Christians have been pressured not only on this front but also by the claims of naturalistic evolution. Metaphysical naturalism (the view that the natural realm is all that there is, and that there is no supernatural realm) and relativism have some core features in common. Taken consistently, both views deny that there are transcendent, universal truths that we can know. Naturalism tends to treat morals as natural, or physical, properties which do not have an immaterial essence to them. Relativism treats morals similarly, by denying their universality. Over time, I think the attacks have taken their toll, and many Christians have become less confident in the unique truth of Christianity. But just the fact that the broader culture advocates and pressures us to be tolerant is not in itself a good reason to be tolerant. The culture could be mistaken.

Two, some Christians think that Jesus Himself taught us not to judge others. After all, they may say, Jesus told us, "Do not judge lest you be judged" (Matt. 7:1). So, the relativist line, "Who are we to judge?" seems to fit with Jesus' own teachings. But the context of Matthew 7 easily refutes this claim. Jesus is not talking about never making moral judgments; rather, He is telling us not to have a critical spirit. When we are to judge, we should first remove the log in our own eye before trying to remove the speck in a brother or sister's eye (vv. 3-5). But note that we *are* to help remove that speck (v. 5). Further in the chapter, Jesus makes moral judgments Himself. He calls certain people hypocrites (v. 5), dogs and swine (v. 6), evil (v. 11), and false prophets and ravenous wolves (v. 15). He also clearly says that not everyone will make it into the kingdom of heaven (vv. 21-23). Jesus did not mean that we should never make judgments, for He Himself did, even in the very context in which some say He told us not to judge.

So far, these are not good reasons to embrace relativism. There is, I think, a third reason why believers tend to accept relativism, but I will wait until the end of the chapter to suggest it. For now, what about the second question? Is moral relativism problematic in its own right, and what about its import for Christians? I should note that Christians have written many good works against relativism.[4] But is all the criticism just from Christians? What do secular people think? Don't they think that relativism is right? Quite the contrary, from my experience, most philosophers realize that relativism is bankrupt. As I mentioned in the introduction, at USC, I would give my students an essay by the secular philosopher Louis Pojman, and though nearly all of my students entered class thinking ethics were relative, nearly all of them changed their minds after reading and discussing his essay.[5] So let me survey a few core reasons he gives to reject relativism. On any account, Christian or secular, ethical relativism is a belief system that should be dismissed.

---

[4] For instance, see Francis J. Beckwith and Greg Koukl, *Relativism: Feet Firmly Planted in Mid-Air* (Grand Rapids, Mich.: Baker, 1998). See also Paul Copan, *True for You, But Not for Me* (Minneapolis: Bethany, 1998).

[5] Louis Pojman, "Ethical Relativism: Who's to Judge What's Right or Wrong?" Chapter 2 in *Ethics: Discovering Right and Wrong*, 2nd ed. (Belmont, Mass.: Wadsworth, 1990).

RELATIVISM IN LIGHT OF SECULAR PHILOSOPHY

First, what exactly is ethical relativism? It is the belief that there are no universal moral values or principles that are true for all people in all times and places. Like postmodernism, ethical relativism depends on the belief that ethical values and principles are just humanly made; that is, they are constructed. But unlike the postmodern views we have seen, relativism *per se* need not hold that we are "inside" our language. Also unlike postmodern views, relativism does *not* presuppose that we cannot *know* if there are objective truths. Instead, it depends on the metaphysical view that there *are no* objective, universally valid moral truths, period. It denies that any such truths exist, which is a stronger, more definite claim than the postmodern one.

Ethical relativism rests on two independent premises. The first is called the *diversity thesis,* which simply states that morals in fact often do vary from society to society. It is a descriptive thesis, one that is based on observation of different peoples' morals. The second thesis is the *dependency thesis,* which holds that moral values or principles are valid if and only if they are accepted as such by either an individual or a cultural group. The former thesis is called *subjectivism,* while the latter is called *conventionalism.*

Since much good work already has been done on this topic, we will only briefly examine these two theses. According to subjectivism, an individual decides what is right for himself or herself, and that is all it takes to make those values or principles right for that person. But as Pojman and many Christian authors have pointed out, this view leads to the complete demise of morality itself. If subjectivism is right, then absurd consequences follow. For instance, Hitler, Stalin, Saddam Hussein, or Pol Pot would be just as moral as Jesus, Gandhi, or Mother Teresa. I should note that my students at USC readily recognized the absurdity of this conclusion. Furthermore, if what is right is just up to us individually, then there is no moral basis for how we should get along in society, and there is no basis for law. There is no moral basis to which we can appeal to properly decide who is right and who is wrong when two people are in conflict. But as Pojman observes, morality is all about the proper resolution of conflicts, and if subjectivism is true, then morality itself goes out the window.[6] All we have left are individuals with their own personal values who collide in the public square. By this view, life would be, in the words of Thomas Hobbes, "nasty, brutish, and short."

Since subjectivism fails, maybe its socially based cousin, conventionalism, can succeed. This view seems more in keeping with our contemporary emphasis on cultural differences, since according to conventionalism morality is just an invention of a given culture. But if this idea were true, more absurd results would follow. First, a moral reformer like Martin Luther King, Jr., or Mother Teresa, would be immoral! They went against what society already had decided was right, and according to conventionalism that societal acceptance made those views right. But that runs counter to our deeply held intuitions about the moral praiseworthiness of such reformers. Jesus Himself would have been immoral (and thus a sinner) for teaching against the Pharisees' interpretations of, and additions to, the Law. That result alone should be reason for Christians to reject this view.

If conventionalism were true, then the Allies, led by the United States, would have been utterly immoral for trying Nazis as criminals at Nuremberg. The U.S. also would be deeply immoral for intervening on behalf of occupied Kuwait in the 1990 Gulf War. Furthermore, the Union would have been immoral for forcing the Confederacy to stop slavery. In short, there would be no moral basis for intervening on behalf of another oppressed people, or for stopping tyrants, even if they were committing genocide. In light of this extremely counterintuitive conclusion, I had only two students over four years' time at USC who still were willing to bite the bullet and maintain the relativist line that if the Nazis believed something was right for them, then that was okay for them.

Let me highlight one other pressing problem for relativism. If relativism were right, then, quite contrary to our cultural mantra that we must be tolerant, there would be no moral basis for being tolerant. If conventionalism were true, then why should a group be tolerant unless its members happen to accept tolerance as a moral virtue? For example, why should neo-Nazis or Skinheads be tolerant of all peoples? I think they should be tolerant because all of us are made in the image of God and are intrinsically valuable to Him. That is, tolerance makes sense if

---

[6] Ibid., 23.

we understand it as respecting people due to our having equal moral value, due to being image bearers of God. But if values are dependent on cultural (or group) acceptance, there is no moral reason why Skinheads or neo-Nazis should tolerate some group they despise. They simply have no moral reason for being tolerant. Yet on our secular campuses, student groups will find out very quickly that unless they are tolerant of a wide range of diverse viewpoints, they will incur the wrath of, and ostracism by, the administration. But on what moral basis can the administration make this kind of move? There is no such basis, since there are no universal values, according to conventionalism. Quite simply, all that a conventionalist can appeal to is power.

For all these reasons and more that even secular philosophers like Pojman have offered, ethical relativism is a bankrupt view of the nature of morality. Despite all the cultural mantras about being tolerant, Christians should not settle for a relativistic kind of tolerance, since that will not succeed in building a moral society or in helping people be moral. Tolerance (i.e., respect for people as having equal moral value) makes sense only if there exists a universal, objective moral truth that we are made in God's image, and that is the truth that those of us in the Judeo-Christian tradition uniquely have. We dare not compromise on that truth.

If relativism and postmodernism fail, their failure alone does not establish that morals are objective. Nor will an appeal to Scripture as the basis for objective moral truth gain much of a hearing from a secular audience. Is there some other way to help demonstrate that morality is objective?

Fortunately, there is, and even Pojman realizes this. On both relativistic and postmodern views, morals end up being basically human inventions. But there are some morals that do not seem to be that kind of thing at all. Consider the following moral principles:

1. Murder is wrong.
2. Rape is wrong.
3. Torturing babies for fun is wrong.
4. Genocide is wrong.
5. Slavery is wrong.

It seems that once we understand the concepts expressed in these statements, we simply see that these acts are wrong. In fact, one time when I was teaching this subject at USC, the campus was sponsoring a "rape awareness" forum. The message was clear: rape is inherently wrong. But in principle, that could not be the case if morals are relative. The same would be true for murder, genocide, and other such behaviors.

Moral relativism claims that there are no universally valid, objective morals that are true for all people at all times. But the above-listed principles seem to be clear counterexamples to that conclusion. If those five principles are universally valid, objective moral truths, then ethical relativism is clearly false.

But maybe there is a reply the relativist can make at this point. I was discussing these very moral truths with a professor at USC, and his reply was instructive. He claimed that, over time, society has simply come to decide that certain things are morally right or wrong. *But if he is right, then it could have been otherwise.* That is, it *could have been* the case that we would have decided that murder, rape, or genocide is not wrong after all. But that possibility is absurd!

So, it surely seems that these moral truths are objectively true after all, and if that is the case, there is at least a core to morality that is universally valid and cannot be relative. Notice that my strategy has been to choose clear-cut examples of moral truths that cannot be relative, and then press the counterintuitive results that follow if we were to say that morality simply is "up to us." These are truths we all can know (and indeed we all should know) are true, and we know them by simple reflection, or intuition. Furthermore, I do not have to give reasons for their being true; they simply are true, and everyone should know that. The burden of proof is on anyone who denies that these things are true.

At this point, I have found that a question frequently arises for Christians: Aren't these moral truths examples of *absolute* truths? Why should we call them *objective* moral truths? Most often, I have seen Christians defending absolute morality versus relativism, as though those were the only two options. Let me now make four distinctions between my use of the terms "absolute" and "objective" morality.

1. *Metaphysically:* What *are* these moral truths? They are not physical things, like the movement of body parts, or just ways of behaving, or even just what most people happen to prefer in a given culture. Those

would be the kinds of ways naturalistic science might try to "operationalize" morals, but these moral truths are not at all those kinds of things. They also are not just expressions of feelings, as emotivists would claim. In such a case, the statement that "murder is wrong" would be something equivalent to the exclamation "Ugh, murder!" No, these moral truths are transcendent, universally valid, immaterial truths that are fundamentally moral in nature. Both *absolute* and *objective* morals have this feature in common.

2. *Epistemologically:* How do we *know* these moral truths? These examples of clear-cut moral truths are known by human reason, or intuition. We simply know them to be valid. There are other truths of reason, such as, "treat equals equally," "keep your promises," and, "do no harm." As Christians, of course, we know that reason takes us only so far. As fallen human beings are capable of suppressing moral truth, so we need an objectively valid standard to help us know what really are moral truths. Thus while reason (or, as many have called it, general revelation, or natural law) is one key way to know moral truths, we also need special revelation (i.e., Scripture). The appeal to reason, of course, helps us apologetically by offering a point of commonality with nonbelievers who do not recognize the authority of Scripture. As a second point, we can know these truths as they really are. That is, we are not cut off from knowing reality, as postmodernists would say. Again, both *absolute* and *objective* morals share this feature.

3. *Scope: Who* is subject to these morals? This is really just emphasizing one aspect I already raised under metaphysical traits, but it bears repeating. Both *absolute* and *objective* morals are valid for all people, in all times, in all places. That is, they are universally valid; no one is exempt from them.

4. *Applicability:* In this fourth and final distinction, we may see a *difference* between absolute and objective morality. Here, the question is: do these morals *apply* in one hundred percent of the cases or not? An absolutist view would maintain that we *always* must obey such morals. But an objectivist might see that in some cases of genuine conflict between two competing moral truths, one may take precedence in moral importance over another, and therefore we should carry out the one with greater moral weightiness.

Allow me to illustrate. Suppose we are in occupied Holland during

World War II, and we are hiding Jews in our basement. One day, Nazi soldiers pound on the door. We open it, and they demand to know if there are any Jews in our house. What should we tell them? Here we are facing a moral conflict. On the one hand, we know that, as a moral truth, we should tell the truth, but we also know that if we admit that there are Jews inside, then most likely, they will be murdered. What do we do? Do we tell the truth, and thereby almost certainly guarantee they will be murdered, or do we lie and try to protect the Jews from being murdered?

A strict absolutist would hold that we always must obey moral truths, and so we must tell the truth. But an objectivist has another option available. He or she could reason that, yes, both moral principles are valid, but they genuinely conflict, and one clearly outweighs the other (protecting the Jews from being murdered is morally more important than telling the truth). In such a case, where there is a genuine conflict, an objectivist can maintain that we should obey the morally more important principle.

But wouldn't we be committing sin by not telling the truth? That is, even if we follow the more important principle, don't we still commit a lesser evil, and thus sin, by lying? One reason why it is not a sin to obey the more important principle in cases of genuine conflict is that, if it were, then we could be in predicaments where there is no way we could *not* sin, and yet we would still be blameworthy before God. But that result does not seem plausible.[7] Second, consider the example from Exodus 1:15-21, where Pharaoh commanded the Hebrew midwives to kill the male babies at birth. Because the midwives feared God, they did not obey Pharaoh. When Pharaoh called them to give an account for their disobedience, they basically told a lie: "Because the Hebrew women are not as the Egyptian women; for they are vigorous, and they give birth before the midwife can get to them" (v. 19). What is especially interesting to me is God's response: "So God was good to the midwives, and the people multiplied, and became very mighty. And it came about because the midwives feared God, that He established households for them" (vv. 20-21). Even though they lied, God blessed them, and there is no suggestion that they had to repent of sin. So it seems that they could

---

[7] For further discussion of this issue, see also Scott B. Rae, *Moral Choices,* 2nd ed. (Grand Rapids, Mich.: Zondervan, 2000), 35. Also, see Norm Geisler's discussion in "Morality, Absolute Nature of," *Baker Encyclopedia of Christian Apologetics* (Grand Rapids, Mich.: Baker, 1999), 501-502.

obey the more important command, while failing to keep the lesser one, and yet not sin.

What does the list of five objective moral truths give us? At this point, by just appealing to intuition, it gives us a core set of moral truths. Again, logically speaking, this is enough to refute ethical relativism, which claims that there are *no* universal, objective morals.

For now, let me draw one very important conclusion. Clearly, ethical relativism is a mistaken view, even on secular grounds. *There is no good reason for Christians to accept it as the whole story of morality.* Yet, we have seen that many Christians do accept it. Why? There is no good rationale for this, as even secularized students can see. But a *third* reason why I think relativism is attractive is that we as Christians have been deeply affected by the surrounding American culture, which has bought the belief that the goal of life is to indulge our desires. This belief stems straight from the attractiveness of sin, and believers are not immune to that allure. Relativism (and/or postmodernism) lets us think we can be in charge.

Therefore, for Christians to accept these views is tantamount to committing adultery against God. When believers persist in embracing relativism, they end up committing adultery against God by buying into a moral philosophy that is utterly opposed to God's revealed truth, whether that is in general revelation (which, as we have seen, even secular people know), or special revelation in Scripture. Relativism also puts us in the idolatrous position of *being God* by deciding what is morally right or wrong. Indeed, Christian postmodernism does the same, in that we end up constructing God by our language, which is plainly idolatrous. So, embracing relativism and/or postmodernism (that is, the points of postmodernism that we have criticized) is a serious matter to God.

Even though there are some good points to learn from Christian postmodernists, we have seen that Christians should not embrace either postmodernism or relativism. I have begun to sketch a basis for our thinking that, contrary to what postmodernists and relativists claim, we can know objective ethical truths that do indeed exist. In the next chapter we will look in some greater detail at reasons why Christians should have confidence in the objective truth of their faith.

"For I want you to know how great a struggle I have on your behalf, and for those who are at Laodicea, and for all those who have not personally seen my face, that their hearts may be encouraged, having been knit together in love, and attaining to all the wealth that comes from the full assurance of understanding, resulting in a true knowledge of God's mystery, that is, Christ Himself, in whom are hidden all the treasures of wisdom and knowledge."

THE APOSTLE PAUL, COLOSSIANS 2:1-3

"And we know that the Son of God has come, and has given us understanding, in order that we might know Him who is true, and we are in Him who is true, in His Son Jesus Christ. This is the true God and eternal life."

THE APOSTLE JOHN, 1 JOHN 5:20

NINE

OBJECTIVE TRUTH: IS THERE SUCH A THING? CAN WE KNOW IT?

In chapter 6, I examined Brian McLaren's description of the modern church's shortcomings, and I suggested that he has misdiagnosed the problem and, thus, the solution. A key factor that I suggested would help solve many of the problems he emphasizes is grace. There I made several suggestions to resolve those problems, such that if we follow them, we do not need to adopt a postmodern way of being a Christian. Those recommendations were:

1. that we don't fall into the trap of thinking that we must have certainty in order to have knowledge (even in our preaching or attitudes);
2. that we practice grace together with truth;
3. that we provide safe places for people to share their souls deeply and thereby connect with one another;
4. that we provide deeply satisfying theological teaching, which engages the intellect and the whole person; and
5. that we really seek to live out the faith in deeply authentic ways, as Jesus' disciples.

In the same spirit of grace, I have suggested that we can embody and express an epistemic humility in our claims about Christianity. By not having to have certainty in order to have knowledge, we are free from overstating the degree of confidence we have in our beliefs. In turn, we will tend to attract postmodern people, who would be put off if we claimed to have utter certainty. We also can rebut the skeptical challenge that arises when we think we must be certain in order to know. But in not requiring certainty in order to know, we still may have a very, very high degree of justification in our beliefs. For instance, at this stage in my life, my beliefs that God exists and that Jesus is the only way to God seem to me to be as basic—as foundational, as certain—as they can get. We may hold our beliefs with an overwhelming amount of justification, so that the burden of proof rests on the one who challenges our belief, and so that, to undercut the evidence in support of our beliefs, the challenger must present very weighty evidence indeed.

All this is by way of reminder. Before we embark on my positive case that we can, and often do, have knowledge of objective truth, I want to underscore how important it is that we do not lose sight of the need to wed together our hearts and our minds. We need to love God with all our hearts, souls, minds, and strength; and we need to love our neighbors as ourselves (Matt. 22:37; Mark 12:30; Deut. 6:5). We need to hold together grace and truth, as did Jesus (John 1:17), who taught and lived the truth in such an attractive, powerful manner that the world has never been the same. Jesus continues to set people free *from* the law, sin, death, their woundedness, themselves, and more. Furthermore, He sets people free *to* love, know, and serve God, have joy, and live authentically, along with so much more.

Let us be mindful of one other caution. People have used claims to have objective truth in ways to oppress others, and we need to be aware that we too can do the same. I found that this was one of the most significant reasons why many of my fellow doctoral students at the University of Southern California had rejected their Catholic upbringing. Instead of embracing the good aspects of their spiritual heritage (e.g., the value of Scripture, that Jesus is God, that He died and rose from the dead to save us from our sins), they rejected it altogether because of what they took to be oppressive attitudes and actions of the Catholic Church hierarchy. A common example would be papal justifications for the Crusades, as though they were commanded by God Himself. Another case would be the control over women, in terms of their roles in the Church. Often, what I saw was that female doctoral students (and even males who had been persuaded by similar reasoning) felt that the Church's hierarchy, instead of proclaiming the will of God, enforced its own particular biases, which were fueled by their own male desires for power and domination.

We may not face the exact same challenges, but we should be mindful that though we are redeemed by Jesus, we too can subtly justify our own prejudices, all in the name of God's revealed, objective will (as we have interpreted it). As an illustration, I have mentioned earlier that we can enforce our own interpretations of what it means to be spiritual. For example, we may believe that to be spiritual, we just need to read Scripture, pray, go to church, confess our sins, and be filled with the Spirit. Or, if we struggle with emotional problems, perhaps even from sexual abuse, we assume that it is our fault, that is, it is due to our own sin and our not trusting God to fix our problems. Further, good Christians should not go see a counselor, even a so-called "Christian" counselor, for to do so is to not trust God to fix us simply by our confessing our sin and His filling us with His Spirit. But as Swindoll points out, such views are part of a shame-based spirituality, not a healthy kind.[1] We can oppress fellow Christians by thus putting them in a box of our own making.

With those cautions in mind, I will begin to explore reasons why I think we can, and often do, know an objective reality as it really is. We can know truth, and we even can know what truth is, i.e., a correspondence with reality. *The importance of this examination cannot be overstated.* Though our postmodern authors presuppose what they deny (our ability to know objective reality), that alone does not show that we do in fact know such truth. So I need to show that we can and often do have such knowledge, in order to finish the other half of my argument.

Even more so, there are other, specific issues at stake. For one, the idea that there are objective moral truths has been under attack vigorously for quite some time, as we have seen already. For another, the idea that there are objective, historical facts has been assaulted and denied, so that under postmodern criticisms it is commonplace to think that there is no such thing as history but only histories, which are made by those who get to write the narrative. That claim has serious implications for the trustworthiness and historical accuracy of the biblical accounts, such as in the Gospels or Acts. Can we know historical facts?

---

[1] Charles Swindoll, *The Grace Awakening* (Nashville: W Publishing Group, 2003), 212-215.

My approach, therefore, will be to sketch a way in which we have knowledge of objective truths in general kinds of cases. To do this, I will examine a series of mundane cases that we may experience in everyday life to show how we do have contact with (and can know) objective reality. Then I will draw upon those cases and develop a theoretical explanation. My concern here, however, is not only to justify my claim that we can and often do have knowledge of objective truth, nor merely to develop a theory for theory's sake. I intend also to apply my claim about objective truth to areas of critical concern, especially as it pertains to Christians and Christianity. So far in this book, I have been addressing two main areas of concern, moral and religious claims, especially since the claims of those areas have been regarded for some time as mere opinions or values and not facts. Since the Bible makes many claims about historical events, I will try to apply my methodology for knowing objective truth to historical claims as well as to moral claims.

OUR KNOWLEDGE OF THE EXTERNAL, OBJECTIVE WORLD

Let us start by examining several cases, mostly everyday kinds of events, to show that we do have access to, and can know, the real world.

The train ticket example: I commute by rail to and from school, and I was struck recently by the awarenesses required to buy and later validate my Metrolink train ticket. When you buy a ticket at the station, you use an electronic vending machine, which walks you through several steps. You have to identify first which kind of ticket you want to buy—one-way, round-trip, ten-trip, or monthly pass. You also have to identify what kind of passenger you are—a child under five years of age, an adult, if you are disabled, etc. Then you have to choose your station of destination. Next, you select payment options—cash, or debit or credit card. Then you enter any card information (e.g., PIN), and then you collect your ticket and receipt.

What is involved at each step? You have in front of you a computer-like display with buttons to push on the sides. You have to see the words on the screen for what they are, and that they match up with a certain button (and not another, which is not always so clearly aligned). Then you have to see that you pressed the button associated with the option you intended to choose. If you get a confusing message on the next screen, you have to see those words for what they are, understand them, and then press the appropriate button, to command the machine to proceed with your request.

Here, you have to see things *for what they are* (e.g., the words), match up other items with them (e.g., buttons), and recognize if you did or did not press the right one. If you did, or even didn't, make a mistake, you can know that by comparing your awarenesses (and memories of them, too) of what button you pushed with what the words say. In all steps, *you have to see the things involved for what they are* and understand what you are trying to do by forming and using concepts (e.g., that to proceed to any next step, you have to press the button matched up with the desired option displayed). Then you can check up on the result by reading the print on your ticket—that it is, say, a ten-trip ticket between that station and the desired destination, comparing it with your intentions—and then either accepting the ticket or seeking to get a refund.

The prescription refill example: In this case, the same sorts of conclusions can be seen as in the preceding example. I use my telephone to call in refills for prescriptions. I bring the drug vial with me to the phone while I call, because I will be prompted by the system to enter certain information, starting with my phone number. I have to look at the phone's keypad, notice which keys are for which numbers, and then press the correct numbers in sequence. How do I (or anyone else) do that? I think of a number, and then I see which key is for that number, and then I direct my finger to that key and press it. After doing that for all the digits, I hear the number played back to me, and again I have to verify that I entered the number correctly. How do I do that? I listen to the digits, one at a time, compare them with my memorized phone number, and then I can compare the numbers spoken back to me in a sequence with those of my phone number. I have to be able to hear the numbers for what they are, compare them with what I know to be my number, and see that they match up.

The same follows when I enter the prescription number, which in turn is repeated back to me. Again, I have to be able to see the number, this time on the vial, *as it really is,* then see which keys are for which numbers, then direct my finger to press the right key. If I make a mistake, I can know that because I see that I pressed the wrong one. So, I must be able to see the numbers for what they are on the vial, then do the same with the keypad, and then match up the audio feedback with the number as I read it on the vial. In all cases, I have to be able to see the numbers for what they are, in order to match them up.

In what I have just described, I can match up my awarenesses with the objects (the keys on the phone, and the numbers imprinted on the prescription label), to see that they match up. Let us continue with further cases, to see what else we may learn.

The example of reading a text aloud: Suppose you are reading a passage of Scripture aloud in your church's worship service, and your passage is Romans 1:16-17:

> For I am not ashamed of the gospel, for it is the power of God for salvation to everyone who believes, to the Jew first and also to the Greek. For in it the love of God is revealed from faith to faith; as it is written, "But the righteous man shall live by faith."

Suppose you read the passage *just like that.* Now, you may notice that some people look up at you with a puzzled look on their faces. You might start to wonder why. Then, maybe someone pulls you aside and, to your surprise, tells you that you read it wrong, that you substituted "love" for "righteousness" in verse 17.

How would anyone present know whether what you read was right or not? Somehow they have to hear the sounds you uttered *for what they are,* see what the word in the passage *actually is,* compare the two, and then express their thoughts properly in language (e.g., "You misread the passage," not, "Great job!"). I did this intentionally in a philosophy class one day to see how attentively they were following my reading, and then to force them to pay attention to their awarenesses—what they heard and what they read, their comparison of the two, and their judgment. How can we ever correct anyone if we do not have access to things as they really are, and if we cannot each see what is indeed the case?

The balls and colors examples: Consider how a child learns the word "ball." In the presence of the child, parents may point at a red ball and utter "ball!" Depending on her age, the child may try to imitate the utterance. But as Wittgenstein notes, pointing at a ball does not guarantee that a child now understands the meaning of "ball" to be associated with the ball; it still could be the case that a child may associate "ball" with the red color, or its texture, and so on. However, on other occasions the parents will repeat the lesson, and often with other balls, say, a white ping pong ball, a basketball, or a baseball. The child sees the red ball, the ping pong ball, the basketball, and so on. After many experiences, the child can develop the ability to call the balls back to memory and compare them. The child then notices what is in common to these objects that makes them all balls. On the basis of that noticing, the child develops the concept of what it is to be a ball, and in so doing, she can understand what it is to be a ball. Then the child can go to a friend's house and see a new, different kind of ball that she has not seen before (for instance, a football) and still be able to label it correctly by the term "ball."

Alternatively, the child may see something (for example, a very round pumpkin or gourd) at a distance, or in a poorly lit area, that is initially taken to be a ball. She may at first refer to it by "ball," but when she comes closer to the pumpkin, she may notice now that it is not a ball. Indeed, it somehow does not fit the concept of a ball that she has developed, and she may not know what to call it, if she does not know the word "pumpkin."

This is how my daughter has developed concepts of various colors, shapes, and fruits. We have a book that has on adjacent pages many pictures of these kinds of things. When she was very young, I would point to a picture, and then I would utter the word for it (e.g., "apple"). Maybe I would then ask her, "Where are the other apples?" and she would point to the other apple pictures. Then I might identify the banana pictures, then oranges, and so forth.

In other settings, like the grocery store, she would see a real red delicious apple, and then she would exclaim "apple!" Then, to vary the example, I would show her a golden delicious apple, or a Gala one, and she could see that it also was an apple. She was able to see an apple itself (even of a different kind), expand her concept of what an apple is, and still label it properly in language.

The veterinarian example: This example is directed particularly against postmodern authors such as Hauerwas, and Kallenberg, whose views on this topic I have examined elsewhere in detail.[2] Imagine that we are in a veterinarian's office. Suppose someone in our veterinarian "community" uses "dog" when something enters the clinic that we have agreed to call "wolf." Somehow the other members of our community need to be able to recognize that this play of the game does not follow the rules. There must be a way for members to check up on that use of language as well as other behaviors, if real communication is to take place at all. Such seeing requires the *same* ability as in the balls, colors, and apples examples, namely, that somehow, each member of the community needs to see the animal in question *for what it is*. Also, a community member needs to see that this animal fulfills the concept of being a dog *before* that person can know that this situation calls for the use of the term "dog," and not "wolf."

The surf fishing example: Suppose there is a community in Carlsbad, California, whose members practice surf fishing. (I speak from within such a community, as such a fisherman, who has participated for decades, and who was trained by other such fishermen.) There are generations of such members. When a newcomer is initiated into the practice, he or she typically first learns to cast with a spinning reel, since with such a reel it is not necessary to think about stopping the forward motion of the line when it hits the water's surface. But with an open-faced reel, the fisherman must carefully monitor the progress of both the line and sinker through the air. Immediately upon hitting the surface of the water, the person must press with the thumb against the reel in order to stop both the line and the spinning of the spool. Otherwise, the spool will continue to turn rapidly, and the line on the reel will peel off and tangle into a "bird's nest," since the motion of the sinker has been drastically slowed by the surf.

There are many other kinds of skills needed to engage in this practice successfully, such as the need to distinguish between a corbina bite and a croaker bite, and even within either kind of bite, the differences between a young small fish's bite and a large adult's bite. *Regardless of the specific skill, what is indispensable to acquiring it, much less fishing with it, is that the individual fisherman must have an awareness that is*

---

[2] E.g., in my *Virtue Ethics and Moral Knowledge: Philosophy of Language After MacIntyre and Hauerwas* (Aldershot, England: Ashgate, 2003), chapter 5.

unavailable to any other member of the surf fishing community. An onlooker, or even a trainer, can judge by a bird's nest that I failed to stop the spool from spinning, but only I can be aware that a certain pressure of the thumb, combined with a certain felt level of effort of my cast, produced a longer cast than one where I pressed slightly more firmly on the spool. In night fishing, this first-person awareness becomes more important, because I must judge by my experience (and not by sight) that once I have cast with a certain degree of strength, released the line at a certain angle, and waited a certain amount of time, I must then stop the reel's spinning.

Consider also how an expert angler trains a new fisherman in when to "set the hook." The expert can describe in words or demonstrate when to pull back on the rod smoothly, yet quickly pull when the rod moves in such-and-such a manner. The novice needs to observe, ask questions, and try to imitate that behavior, but ultimately, what both fishermen require is a keen awareness of the felt quality of both the bite and the resultant tug on the line. Regardless of any onlooker's understanding of the motions, each fisherman (expert or beginner) needs not *just* a know-how of fishing, something that could be described in third-person terms. Indispensably, the good fisherman must *also* have experience with fishing that allows him or her to distinguish between the felt qualities of each bite, whether it is just a beginning nibble, a bite that will allow him or her to hook the fish, or some other kind of bite. The individual person must pay attention to his or her awarenesses and learn to distinguish between slight variations in similar kinds of experiences. This is why a more experienced angler can train another fisherman in all the relevant tips, strategies, and motions, but still be a better fisherman who catches more fish precisely because he or she pays closer attention to the felt qualities of, and minute distinctions between, bites, wave actions, and more.

So, it is the *good* fisherman who is able to master the requisite skills and thereby achieve expertise in fishing. The good fisherman somehow needs to *see* that this particular case (a certain bite) is an example of a certain kind of bite (for example, that of an adult halibut), and that that kind of bite requires such-and-such action, as opposed to the kind of action required with a bite that is very similar, yet different. It also is entirely possible for someone in this practice to act in the correct manner and yet not truly be skilled. More generally, the excellent fisherman must *see* that C is indeed the case, and that C calls for action A. Indeed, this also seems to be the way other participants in the game also would know that A is appropriate. They too each need to see that C obtains in order to be able to correct the fisherman's actions. *Once again, access to the actual state of affairs, and attention to our intentional awarenesses in order to know the actual state of affairs, are crucial.*

What should we make of these examples? What is going on? Consider again the case of my daughter learning to label her awareness of an apple with the right word. She has to be able to see an apple (for example, a red delicious one) *for what it is.* From many noticings of apples, she develops a concept of what an apple is. She also must see that a particular object of her awareness is another instance of an apple (perhaps a golden delicious one, or maybe a Granny Smith). She learned to associate a term with her awareness of the object by *hearing the term for what it is,* and *seeing the object for what it is,* and then she could compare them and see that, yes, this object is indeed an apple. Alternatively, she could see that it was not an orange, which I could tell by her saying, "Nooo!" if I asked her if the object was an orange.

In the fishing example, the good fisherman needs to be able to experience the felt qualities of wave actions, particular kinds of bites, and more for what they actually are, to know how to react. The good fisherman experiences such things for what they are, and he or she can compare those experiences with his or her understanding of such a thing, to see if they match up.

Before I try to explain how we can know reality, let me try to clarify a few terms I will use in that explanation. First, a *thought* is a mental entity, as opposed to a physical one, and fundamentally it is "a mental content that can be expressed in an entire sentence and that only exists while it is being thought."[3] Second, we also have *sensations.* According to J. P. Moreland and Scott B. Rae, "a *sensation* is a state of awareness or sentience, a mode of consciousness."[4] Some sensations are experiences of things outside of us, while others are awarenesses of internal states. Importantly, both thoughts and sensations (as well as other men-

---

[3] J. P. Moreland and Scott B. Rae, *Body and Soul* (Downers Grove, Ill.: InterVarsity Press, 2000), 158.
[4] Ibid. (emphasis in original).

tal entities, such as beliefs and emotions) have *intentionality*, which simply is their ofness and aboutness. For instance, a feeling is *about* something; some people have the fear *of* heights. Also a thought is *about* something; for instance, I can think about Richard Nixon as president. So, intentionality is a feature, a quality, a property of mental entities.

Some mental entities, though not all, have a *concept* as a feature, or quality. For instance, thoughts and beliefs have concepts, whereas sensations do not. Crucially, concepts are intentional qualities of mental entities such as thoughts and beliefs, so they are of or about things.

While some mental entities (thoughts, sensations, etc.) are of real objects in the world, other mental entities may be of, or about, things that may not actually exist. For instance, I can think of the winged horse Pegasus, even though Pegasus does not actually exist in the real world. The *intensional* qualities (note the different spelling of "intensional," as opposed to "intentional") are features or properties *of the objects* of our mental entities, whether or not those objects actually exist. And, if they do exist, then those actual objects are part of the *extension* of the concept. For example, I can have an awareness of an apple. That awareness has intentionality, which is of the intensional properties of the apple itself. The specific apple is part of the extension of actual apples.

Dallas Willard explains that all of us do this kind of matching up of concepts with the objects of our awarenesses all the time, and that even those who deny that we can do it still engage in doing it.[5] How does this happen? There is a natural affinity between thoughts (which have concepts) and the objects of those thoughts, *due to their natures*. Due to its nature, the concept of an apple has a natural affinity with the properties apples must have in order to be apples. The properties that an apple must have in order to be an apple are its intensional properties, and apples themselves make up the extension of the concept (that is, they are actual apples). So the nature of a concept of an apple is to be of apples. As Willard puts it,

> There is an infinitely rich field of "natural signs," as Thomas Reid called them, entities [i.e., concepts] which immediately carry the mind

[5] Dallas Willard, "How Concepts Relate the Mind to Its Objects: The God's Eye View Vindicated?" *Philosophia Christi* 1:2 (1999): 18.

which exemplifies them to something else [their intensions, and, by extension, to objects that have those intensional properties] because in their nature they inherently involve something else (their specific objects). These are the mental qualities we call concepts.[6]

As Willard illustrates,

A thought of an apple
    (exemplifies/has present in it)
        a concept of apple
            (which has a natural affinity with)
                properties making up "appleness"
                    (which are exemplified in)
                        actual apples.[7]

Three *utterly crucial* points arise. First, Willard observes that

A primary manifestation of the affinity between thought and object is the fact that no one ever has to be taught what their thought (or perception) is a thought (or perception) *of*, nor could they be, though of course they have to learn language for talking about their thought and its objects, and they also have much to learn about thought and its objects. But the child knows what its thoughts (perceptions, etc.) are of as soon as it becomes aware that it is having experiences; and that is one foundation of most other learning that transpires.

Of course I do not mean that further learning is an explicitly logical process, but it is by and large dependent upon the child being able to identify experiences, and thereby what they are of. The child (or adult) has to be able to identify when it is experiencing the same thing or something different. And we do not, for the most part, even know what it would be like to have to identify the child's—or any one else's—experiences for *them*, or teach them how to do it if they did not already know.[8]

---

[6] Ibid., 15. See also Thomas Reid, *An Inquiry into the Human Mind, on the Principles of Common Sense*, ed. Derek R. Brookes (London: Cadell, 1785, 4th ed.; reprint, Bristol: Thoemmes, 1990), chapter 4.
[7] Willard, "How Concepts Relate the Mind to Its Objects," 16.
[8] Ibid., 14-15 (my emphasis is underlined).

This is the pattern I have observed in my little girl. I could not identify her experiences for her; she alone can do that. She has a privileged access to her experiences, and while I can have the same experience (of a thought, concept, etc., which are universals), I cannot have her *having* of it (which is particular). I can pay attention to my own experiences and awarenesses, and then even label them with words, but she has to be able to experience the same thing and be aware of it, or else I would not be able to teach her. If Willard is right, and it surely seems that he is, then it is our own, first-person access to our awarenesses (with their intentional properties) that allow us to identify what our thoughts (with their concepts) are *of*.

Second, *our thoughts, and thus our concepts, do not confer any new properties upon or modify their objects.* How so? Importantly, in general intensional properties, at least of objects in the world, are *not* in the mind, whereas inten*t*ional properties (which are concepts) *are* in the mind, and thus these two kinds of properties are *not* identical. (Again, note the differing spelling of "intensional" and "inten*t*ional," which I am highlighting in italics.) If intensional properties of the objects of my awareness were in my mind, then when I had a thought of Floppsy, one of our old rabbits, I would have a little Floppsy in my mind. My concept of rabbits, and the concept specifically of Floppsy, are not the same as the properties rabbits must have to be rabbits, and for Floppsy to be himself. Rather, rabbits' intensional properties come to mind in my thought of them. In this way, concepts are the intentional bridge between thought and its objects. Now, consider Pegasus: I can have the concept of Pegasus, and my thoughts are of Pegasus, and not the story about it. My concept of Pegasus reaches the intensional properties Pegasus *would* have *if* it existed. But since it doesn't exist, my thought gets no further.

If a thought has a certain concept, which is an inten*t*ional property, then that property has a natural affinity with the properties that make up (or would make up, if they existed) the intension of the concept. In this way, a thought that has a certain concept is (inten*t*ionally) *of* its intension (and thus its extension, real or not). These two kinds of properties are "together" in such a way that the intensional properties "come to mind" whenever that concept is instanced in a thought. But, and this is crucial: the intensional properties are not instanced *in* the thought with that concept.[9]

But, some may ask, how do we know this? This leads to a third crucial point: *we each can compare the object as it is given in experience, with our concept of that object, to see if they match up. I can see if they match up or not, and I can see if my thought of that thing does (or does not do) anything to modify that thing.* This is where I think we must pay very close attention to our awarenesses, for I think we can compare our concepts with things in the world, which can be given in experience, and we can see that they are different, and that my thought (or, awareness, or language use) does not modify its object. We do this all the time; for example, my little girl can compare the apple-as-before-her-mind with her concept of the apple. She does this by seeing if her concept of an apple matches up with the object, and then she can see that it is indeed an apple. If it is (or isn't) as represented, she can observe that, and say, "Apple!" (if her concept and awareness match up), or exclaim, "Orange!" if instead it is an orange. This ability demonstrates a commonsense understanding, namely, that my daughter, along with most adults, takes for granted that her thoughts don't modify objects. In the same way, in the fishing example we can compare our concept of a bite with the bite given in experience. As Willard puts it, "in fact we do this sort of thing [seeing if our concepts match up with objects] all the time, whenever we look at something to see if it is as we have thought it to be."[10] Indeed, as he argues, even those who deny such access to the real world do this all the time, yet they additionally hold that in thinking, seeing, or mentally acting upon some object, we modify it, such that we cannot have access to the real thing in itself. But this is nonsense, as the very ability to have access to reality is presupposed in the denial that we can have such access. The way to show that this is nonsense is by paying close attention to our awarenesses, carefully describing them, and then showing (1) what must be taking place; and (2) that this very ability to know reality must be presupposed by its detractors, in order for them to deny it. But that result undercuts the *entire* constructivist project.

Now, let me consider two other classes of examples, moral and his-

---

[9] See ibid., 15.
[10] Ibid., 18.

torical kinds of cases, to show that we have epistemic access to objectively real moral truths, as well as historical ones.

Moral cases: Immediately, it might seem that regardless of which moral principles or virtues I may choose, they can be disputed. So, let me return to what I think are clear-cut, self-evident moral truths, ones that, as a professor once said, are "settled now." These are ones that Pojman offered in his refutation of relativism, such as murder is wrong; rape is wrong; genocide is wrong; or torturing infants for fun is wrong.

These things seem self-evident to us, despite the fact that I have had people claim that in other tribal cultures (such as the cannibalistic Sawi people, as described by Don Richardson) they might not hold such truths. Others can claim that they do not think these things necessarily are wrong. Yet, I think when they do make such assertions, they either are putting on a mask, to play a role à la Nietzsche, just to see what others will say; or, when pressed, they will quickly abandon such a position. For example, what if we threatened to murder them, or a loved one? Would they just say, "Well, that is okay for you, if you accept it as true"? I *highly* doubt it. Indeed, these moral principles have such an extremely high degree of justification that the burden of proof is on the one who denies that they are true.

But can we get more mileage out of these moral truths? Let us consider the phenomenology involved with our learning what, for example, murder or rape is. Sadly, someday my little girl will have to learn what murder is. At age two, she already is exposed to death through animated movies (for example, the death of Simba's father in *The Lion King*). How will she (or anyone) acquire the concept of murder? I think it will proceed similarly to our other examples, through many noticings and then forming the concept. We become aware of examples of killing, and we learn to distinguish a species of it, murder, by paying attention to our awarenesses (maybe through face-to-face examples, pictures, real-life stories, animated movies or television shows, news reports, etc.), and then forming the concept.

Here is what I think will take place: *once someone forms the concept of murder, that person should immediately see that such an act is wrong, period.* We each can (and should) see that it is a heinous act, a violation of the most repugnant sort, which simply is wrong. If someone seems to grasp the concept, but doesn't see that it is wrong, we wonder what is defective with his or her soul. Indeed, we may well think that the person doesn't truly grasp the concept (for example, maybe the person needs to distinguish between killing and murder). We try to help that person be sure he or she gets the concept by repeating the process involved in acquiring concepts and making more careful distinctions.

Furthermore, as I argued earlier, no one wants to relativize such moral truths so that it would be okay for *that person* to be murdered. If someone claimed that, we would think that person was mentally ill. While some cultures may approve of some forms of killing (for instance, the cannibalism of the Sawi), that doesn't mean that they would approve of murder. I think the best way to explain the Sawi case is that they do not see that form of killing as an act of murder. But from that it does not follow at all that they do not affirm that murder is wrong. All we need is a different case to surface that could show us (as outsiders) that they do indeed affirm that murder is wrong.

I think the truth (and justifiedness) of these clear-cut moral principles is accessible to each of us, unless we are mentally ill, unconscious, or otherwise debilitated. This is what we should expect to be the case if these principles are universals, which they surely seem to be. And if they are universals, and we can and do have access to the real world, then these are remarkably clear instances of objective truths we can know.

It should not seem remarkable that we can know such truths as they really are, especially if the three principles of the "received epistemic heritage" viewpoint are false. Elsewhere, I argued that these three principles are: (1) universals (truths, properties) are not present before the mind; (2) the mind's contact with the world is one of making, not matching; and (3) for a term to succeed in referring, the object of our cognition must exist.[11] But we now have reasons to reject all three of these principles. Contrary to number 1, we can and do experience universals as being present before the mind. *Pace* number 2, we also have seen that the mind's contact with the world is one of matching, not making/constructing. And, against number 3, in cases of "intentional inexistence," the object of our mental states need not exist (as in the case of Pegasus). Rather, cases of intentional inexistence demonstrate what would be the case if such a thing were to exist, even though it does not.

---

[11] See my *Virtue Ethics and Moral Knowledge*, chapter 2.

Historical cases: How does this epistemology play out in terms of historical facts? Alasdair MacIntyre, who is a fountainhead for the thought of Kallenberg, Hauerwas, and Murphy, thinks that facts (that is, truths about objective states of affairs) are a seventeenth-century invention, just like wigs for gentlemen.[12] But that conclusion follows *only if* the so-called "facts" are constructed by our language use, which I have argued does not follow. Can we therefore know facts in the world?

I see no reason why historical facts should be exempt from my previous defense of epistemological realism. Indeed, historical facts seem to be the very thing that we can know in the way I have described, since we are not "cut off" from the real world. What then do we make of events such as Jesus' crucifixion and resurrection? Can we know those facts for what they are? Or, can we know the facts of the matter of who wrote various books of the Bible?

I think the methodology to adopt to answer these and other fact-related questions is the same as we have discussed. For example, how do we determine whether the checkbook is on the table? We look and see; we put ourselves in a condition and place to be able to examine the table and see its contents, and compare those awarenesses with our concepts of the table and checkbook. To do that, I may need to put my glasses on, or take off my dark sunglasses, or turn on the light, or come closer to the table.

How do we verify that Jesus rose from the dead? We examine the evidence and see if the actual states of affairs match up with our concepts. If Jesus rose, then we should find certain things to be the case: for example, we compare the facts (including documentary evidences) with our concepts and see if they match up. Also, the resurrection should be the best explanation to fit the facts. Does this mean that theories have no influence on this process? No; as one example, the Jesus Seminar's naturalism undoubtedly has a crucial impact on their conclusions. But on my view, and Willard's, we can compare theories (including naturalism and the resurrection hypothesis) with reality and see if they match up. The same kind of thought would apply to verifying that 9/11's events really

---

[12] Alasdair MacIntyre, *Whose Justice? Which Rationality?* (Notre Dame, Ind.: University of Notre Dame Press, 1988), 357.

occurred: we examine the evidence (pictures, testimonies, and more), and compare them with our concepts, to see if they match up or not.

Let me illustrate this way of verifying historical events in light of four basic facts about the canonical Gospels.[13] The early church required these criteria for their acceptance of any so-called "Gospel," and accordingly various letters (such as the "secret Gospels") were not regarded as authoritative. The first is that their message represented eyewitness testimony. John writes in 1 John 1:1-2 that he was writing (even in his Gospel) about what the apostles (who were eyewitnesses) had seen and even touched concerning the Word of Life, Jesus. Second, what they reported was public, not private, knowledge. Paul illustrates this in Acts 26:25-26, where he gave his defense before Festus and Agrippa. There, Paul appeals to public knowledge of events that took place, ones that were verifiable.

Third, they appealed to external events (ones that took place objectively, in time and space), and not experiences, ones that would have been private to the one having the internal experiences. Paul writes this way in 1 Corinthians 15:3-8 about the resurrection, remarking that Jesus' death, burial, and resurrection were verifiable by large numbers of witnesses as something that actually took place. Luke also writes in such a way, giving much attention to historical detail. And, fourth, they treated other interpretations as deviant. In Galatians 1:6ff., Paul declares that any gospel other than the one he preached to them is anathema. In 2 Peter 1:16-21, Peter says that he did not follow cleverly devised tales, but instead he gave an account as an eyewitness of Jesus' majesty. Clearly, the New Testament writers such as the apostles Paul, John, and Peter (on whose teaching Mark depended for his Gospel), along with Luke, all appealed to objectively knowable facts in ways that invited investigation into their historicity. They were concerned to give evidence that anyone could investigate and thereby prove to be the truth of the matter.

If it is obvious how to verify facts and truths, why then do we have such widespread adherence to constructivist thought? I think it is for a few reasons. First, we have been influenced for centuries to think that we just cannot know things as they really are, so now it has become commonplace to think that is so. Second, it puts *us* in charge. No one

---

[13] I am indebted to Dr. Gary Inrig of Trinity Evangelical Free Church, Redlands, California, for these insights in his sermon given on August 15, 2004.

has to bow the knee to anything (or any *One*) that is not under our control. That is highly seductive for sinful people, even Christians. Third, as Willard observes, constructivism has been allowed to reign due to a massive misdescription of consciousness. In postmodern authors, for example, there is a dearth (or utter lack) of careful descriptions of what is going on in consciousness when the mind apprehends something. These authors never bother to give us a description of how the mind supposedly constructs its objects by language use. I think it all is due to a poor (or utter lack of) description of what takes place in consciousness when we are aware of something.

CONCLUSION

As I wrap up this book, let me underscore a few key points. First, I have tried to show that some Christians (like McLaren) think a legalistic approach to the faith is due to a modern way of being a Christian. The solution, therefore, is to become a new, postmodern kind of believer. But that conclusion does not follow. We need to be like Jesus, who was full of *both* grace and truth. These must go hand in hand. We need to hold fast to objective truth, which I have tried to show we can and often do know. If we do embody grace and truth, our lives will be like a fragrant aroma to those around us—something that is so needed in a day when people think they have heard it all about Christianity and have found it wanting.

Second, despite my criticisms of postmodernism, I am not saying that all claims by postmoderns are to be rejected. As but one quick example, Jones is right that we need to be very missions-minded in how we contextualize the gospel to reach postmoderns. However, I also have tried to show that Christians should not embrace a postmodern understanding of the faith itself. That will lead to disaster, for Christianity cannot survive a transformation into being a construction of our language use.

Third, Christians need to stop embracing relativism and even a postmodernization of the faith itself, for those attitudes and actions are *adulterous* against God. In effect, even if unconsciously, we set ourselves up as being in control, as being able actually to construct God. That is sin and *cannot* please God.

As one last point, I want to draw out an implication. Can we have accurate experience of God as He actually is, and know it to be such?

Without going into an argument from religious experience, I should point out that on the view I am advocating, yes, it is quite possible to have experience of God and know it to be just that.[14] How would we know that? We would need criteria to assess any putative experience of God, and here is where Scripture would be necessary, as a way to assess our experience against an objective standard. Since we can know things as they are (although not necessarily fully or infallibly), we would compare the experience with what Scripture says and means (which we can know through good interpretation). Scripture would provide checks upon experience and experience claims, as it should.

While our Christian postmodern authors have many good insights for us to consider, there simply is no good reason to give up the historic, orthodox Christian position that we can and indeed often do know objective truth, and that it has been revealed to us in general and special revelation. Survival of the Christian faith (at least in this culture) may well depend on our holding fast to that truth.

---

[14] As one resource, see J. P. Moreland's *Scaling the Secular City* (Grand Rapids, Mich.: Baker, 1987), 231-240.

BIBLIOGRAPHY
AND
FURTHER RESOURCES

A = Advanced, I = Intermediate, B = Beginning

POSTMODERNISM, GENERALLY

Philosophy:

Derrida, Jacques. *Speech and Phenomena.* Evanston: Northwestern University Press, 1973. Derrida rejects the central teachings of his mentor, Edmund Husserl, and develops his own views. Note, though, that it is Husserl's views that have influenced Willard's and my solution to securing objective truth. (A)

Lyotard, Jean-François. *The Postmodern Condition: A Report on Knowledge.* Theory and History of Literature Series. Edited by Wlad Godzich and Jochen Schulte-Sasse. Minneapolis: University of Minnesota Press, 1993. This work is one that many authors keep returning to, in which Lyotard describes postmodernism as an incredulity toward metanarratives. Whether Christianity is a metanarrative or not is a subject of dispute among many postmodern Christian authors. (A)

Wittgenstein, Ludwig. *Philosophical Investigations.* 3rd ed. Edited by G. E. M. Anscombe and Rush Rhees. Translated by G. E. M. Anscombe. New York: Macmillan, 1958. This is one of the later Wittgenstein's foremost works. (A)

Ethics:

MacIntyre, Alasdair. *After Virtue.* 2nd ed. Notre Dame, Ind.: University of Notre Dame Press, 1984. This is one of the most influential texts in the last twenty years, at least in terms of the number of disciplines that have been influenced by it. MacIntyre sets out to understand the nature of the moral mess we are in, and offers his solutions (a recovery of Aristotle's virtue ethics, albeit with significant modifications). (A)

———. *Three Rival Versions of Moral Enquiry.* Notre Dame, Ind.: University of Notre Dame Press, 1990. This is MacIntyre's next book after *Whose Justice? Which Rationality?* He continues to develop the same themes. (A)

———. *Whose Justice? Which Rationality?* Notre Dame, Ind.: University of Notre Dame Press, 1988. This is the sequel to *After Virtue,* and MacIntyre attempts to unpack his theory of tradition-dependent rationality. His hero now has become Thomas Aquinas, so MacIntyre has migrated to a form of Christianity. (A)

EMERGING CHURCH

(Note: I am not trying to give an exhaustive list of books and resources in this category. There are many more than what I have listed. Rather, I am trying to give a representation of several authors, sources, and topics.)

Emergent Village. www.emergentvillage.com.

Jones, Tony. *Postmodern Youth Ministry.* Grand Rapids, Mich.: Zondervan/Youth Specialties, 2001. (B, I)

Kimball, Dan. *The Emerging Church.* Grand Rapids, Mich.: Zondervan, 2003.

McLaren, Brian D. *A Generous Orthodoxy.* Grand Rapids, Mich.: Zondervan/Youth Specialties, 2004. McLaren extends a number of themes and concepts he developed initially in *A New Kind of Christian* and *The Story We Find Ourselves In.* (I)

———. *The Last Word and the Word After That.* San Francisco: Jossey-Bass, 2003. This book is a sequel to *The Story We Find Ourselves In.*

———. *More Ready Than You Realize.* Grand Rapids, Mich.: Zondervan, 2002. (B)

———. *A New Kind of Christian.* San Francisco: Jossey-Bass, 2001. (B)

———. *The Story We Find Ourselves In.* San Francisco: Jossey-Bass, 2003. This book is a sequel to *A New Kind of Christian.* (B)

———. www.anewkindofchristian.com. This is McLaren's own website.

McLaren, Brian D., and Tony Campolo. *Adventures in Missing the Point: How the Culture-Controlled Church Neutured the Gospel.* Grand Rapids, Mich.: Zondervan, 2003.

Sweet, Leonard, ed. *The Church in Emerging Culture: Five Perspectives.* Grand Rapids, Mich.: Zondervan, 2003. This book features an exchange between contributors such as Andy Crouch, McLaren, Erwin Raphael McManus, Michael Horton, and Frederica Matthewes-Green.

Tomlinson, Dave. *The Post-Evangelical.* Revised North American edition. Grand Rapids, Mich.: Zondervan/emergentYS, 2003.

Webber, Robert E. *The Younger Evangelicals: Facing the Challenges of the New World.* Grand Rapids, Mich.: Baker, 2002.

Youth Specialties. www.youthspecialties.com.

CHRISTIAN POSTMODERNISM, PHILOSOPHICAL AND THEOLOGICAL

Brown, Warren S., Nancey Murphy, and H. Newton Malony, eds. *Whatever Happened to the Soul?* Minneapolis: Fortress, 1998. Murphy's views on how to reconceive Christianity in a linguistic approach (à la Austin and Wittgenstein) get further treatment in a text featuring mainly Fuller professors from disciplines such as theology, philosophy, and psychology. In her chapters, she is clear in her rejection of the soul as an entity, and she advocates an understanding of it simply as a way of talking. (A)

Grenz, Stanley. *A Primer on Postmodernism.* Grand Rapids, Mich.: Eerdmans, 1996. Grenz surveys a broad range of topics, including what is postmodernism, how it arose, what is the postmodern ethos, who are the main persons behind it, and how the gospel fits in a postmodern context. (I)

Grenz, Stanley, and John Franke. *Beyond Foundationalism: Shaping Theology in a Postmodern Context.* Louisville: Westminster/John Knox, 2001. (I, A)

Hauerwas, Stanley. *Against the Nations.* Minneapolis: Winston, 1985. (I)

————. *Character and the Christian Life.* San Antonio: Trinity University Press, 1975; reprint, Notre Dame, Ind.: University of Notre Dame Press, 1994. (I)

————. *Christian Existence Today: Essays on Church, World, and Living in Between.* Durham, N.C.: Labyrinth, 1988. (I)

————. "The Church's One Foundation Is Jesus Christ Her Lord; Or, In a World Without Foundations: All We Have Is the Church." In *Theology Without Foundations: Religious Practice and the Future of Theological Truth,* ed. Stanley Hauerwas, Nancey Murphy, and Mark Nation. Nashville: Abingdon, 1994. (I, A)

————. *A Community of Character.* Notre Dame, Ind.: University of Notre Dame Press, 1981. (I)

————. *Dispatches from the Front: Theological Engagements with the Secular.* Durham, N.C.: Duke University Press, 1994. (I)

————. *In Good Company: The Church as Polis.* Notre Dame, Ind.: University of Notre Dame Press, 1995. (I)

————. *The Peaceable Kingdom.* Notre Dame, Ind.: University of Notre Dame Press, 1983. (I)

————. *Unleashing the Scripture: Freeing the Bible from Captivity to America.* Nashville: Abingdon, 1993. (I)

————. *Vision and Virtue.* Notre Dame, Ind.: Fides, 1974; reprint, Notre Dame, Ind.: University of Notre Dame Press, 1981. (I, A)

————. "Why the Truth Demands Truthfulness: An Imperious Engagement with Hartt." *Why Narrative?* Edited by Stanley Hauerwas and L. Gregory Jones. Grand Rapids, Mich.: Eerdmans, 1989: 303-310. (I)

———. *Wilderness Wanderings: Probing Twentieth-Century Theology and Philosophy*. Boulder, Colo.: Westview, 1997. (I)

Hauerwas, Stanley, and David B. Burrell. *Truthfulness and Tragedy*. Notre Dame, Ind.: University of Notre Dame Press, 1977. (I)

Hauerwas, Stanley, and William H. Willimon. *Resident Aliens*. Nashville: Abingdon, 1989. (B)

———. *Where Resident Aliens Live: Exercises for Christian Practice*. Nashville: Abingdon, 1996. (B)

Kallenberg, Brad J. *Ethics as Grammar*. Notre Dame, Ind.: University of Notre Dame Press, 2001. (A) This is a very well-titled book. It is a very sophisticated treatment of the language-world relationship, and he shows that Hauerwas really is Wittgensteinian. Kallenberg gives extensive, detailed treatment of both Wittgenstein's and Hauerwas's views. It also is an attempt to get others to see the world as he does. (A)

———. *Live to Tell*. Grand Rapids, Mich.: Brazos, 2003. This is an apologetic for postmodern types of ministry, as well as a different understanding of witnessing and conversion, in light of postmodern influences in culture. (B, I)

Murphy, Nancey. *Anglo-American Postmodernity*. Boulder, Colo.: Westview, 1997. This is a technical, philosophical work that attempts to address the major philosophical lines of thought needed to develop an Anglo-American version of postmodernism, versus a Continental kind, which would follow people like Derrida. In this book, Murphy gives a detailed treatment of how theology should be the queen of the sciences in a hierarchy of the languages of the other disciplines. She also develops her non-reductive physicalism. (A)

———. *Beyond Liberalism and Fundamentalism: How Modern and Postmodern Philosophy Set the Theological Agenda*. Rockwell Lecture Series. Harrisburg, Pa.: Trinity Press International, 1996. This work looks at Murphy's three-fold approach to postmodern thought along the lines of epistemology, philosophy of language, and metaphysics. She includes in this work the basics of her thought for a Christian approach to a holistic worldview. (A)

———. *Theology in the Age of Scientific Reasoning*. Ithaca, N.Y.: Cornell University Press, 1990. This is the book version of Murphy's second dissertation. The views of Imre Lakatos allow Murphy to unpack her own views of philosophy of science and later apply them to theology and ethics when considered as sciences in their own right. (A)

Murphy, Nancey, Brad J. Kallenberg, and Mark Nation, ed. *Virtues and Practices in the Christian Tradition*. Harrisburg, Pa.: Trinity Press International, 1997 (Note: reprint edition is published by University of Notre Dame Press, 2003). This book is an exposition of several Christian virtues and "practices" (such as witnessing and worship) in light of the influence of Alasdair MacIntyre. The first chapter is by Kallenberg, who gives a masterful synthesis of MacIntyre's main ideas. (A)

Penner, Myron, ed. *Christianity and the Postmodern Turn*. Grand Rapids, Mich.: Brazos, 2005. (I, A) This book will include essays from those more sympathetic with postmodernism (John Franke, Merold Westphal, and J. K. A. Smith), and those not so favorable toward it (Kevin Vanhoozer, Doug Geivett, and myself). It includes an initial chapter from each contributor, as well as a second chapter of responses to each other. In addition, while I have not explicitly replied in this book to Franke's, Westphal's, and J. K. A. Smith's criticisms of my arguments, nonetheless I have addressed them in various ways. In regards to my depiction of being "inside" language (which Franke takes up), I have given a broader sense of that concept in chapter 2. Westphal mistakes the way I depict my lead-off argument, the presupposition of epistemic access, in chapter 5. Finally, Smith argues that all experience involves interpretation. But I have tried to give numerous examples in chapter 9 to show that while interpretation is very important, nonetheless we can (and often do) have direct experience of reality, as it really is, without interpretation. (I, A)

CRITIQUES OF POSTMODERNISM AND THE EMERGING CHURCH

Carson, D. A. *Becoming Conversant with the Emerging Church: Understanding a Movement and Its Implications*. Grand Rapids, Mich.: Zondervan, 2005. Carson details some strengths of the Emerging Church, and he develops several detailed criticisms of Emerging Church leaders (in particular, Brian McLaren) that focus on biblical, historical, and theological issues. (I)

Erickson, Millard. "The Challenge of Postmodernism." Lecture given at Biola University for the Defending the Faith Lecture Series. This taped lecture is available through Biola University's Apologetics program. (B, I)

———. *The Postmodern World*. Wheaton, Ill.: Crossway, 2002. Erickson addresses postmodernism for a lay audience, with some implications drawn out of postmodernism for Christians. He focuses on Derrida, Rorty, Foucault, and others as his examples. (B)

———. *Postmodernizing the Faith: Evangelical Responses to the Challenge of Postmodernism*. Grand Rapids, Mich.: Baker, 1998. Erickson examines a range of representatives of the faith, such as those who reply negatively to postmodernism (Thomas Oden, Francis Schaeffer, and David Wells), those who reply positively (Grenz, J. Richard Middleton and Brian Walsh, and B. Keith Putt), and then offers his own final chapter. (I)

———. *Truth or Consequences: The Promise and Perils of Postmodernism*. Downers Grove, Ill.: InterVarsity Press, 2002. Of his three books on postmodernism, this is the most academic. He examines mainly Continental philosophers, such as Derrida and Foucault, as well as Richard Rorty and Stanley Fish, and he finds both strengths and weaknesses to postmodernism. He also suggests where he thinks philosophy will go after postmodernism. (I, A)

Groothuis, Doug. *Truth Decay*. Downers Grove, Ill.: InterVarsity Press, 2000. Groothuis gives an extended, important examination of the issues of postmodernism, especially in terms of attacks on the concept of truth as absolute, objective, and universal. He examines a broad range of topics, such as the biblical view of truth; the postmodern challenge to theology; dangers to avoid in apologetics; how to conduct apologetics to postmoderns; ethics; beauty; and race and gender. (I)

Honeysett, Marcus. *Meltdown*. Grand Rapids, Mich.: Kregel, 2004. Honeysett carefully examines and critiques the thought of Derrida, Baudrillard, Foucault, and Butler and their influence on culture.

Smith, R. Scott. "Christian Postmodernism and the Internal Relation of Language and the World." In *Christianity and the Postmodern Turn*, ed. Myron Penner. Grand Rapids, Mich.: Brazos, 2005. I focus on what I think is the main issue in postmodernism, philosophically speaking, and I argue that Grenz, Franke, Hauerwas, and Kallenberg all presuppose what they deny, that we can and often do have access to know the objective world. I also discuss the issue that, on this view, we end up being idolaters by constructing God. (I)

————. "Defusing Intellectual Time Bombs in the Church." Lecture given at Biola University, March 2003, for the Defending the Faith Lecture Series. This taped lecture is available through Biola University's Apologetics program. I survey what postmodernism is all about, in terms of the "street" and academic versions, and then I develop a few main lines of criticism. (B, I)

————. "Hauerwas and Kallenberg, and the Issue of Access to an Extra-Linguistic Realm." *Heythrop Journal*, 45:3, July 2004. This is a technical assessment of their view that we cannot know an objective realm. Then I begin to sketch what a positive case might look like, to show how we do indeed have knowledge of an objective realm. (A)

————. "Language, Theological Knowledge, and the Postmodern Paradigm." In *Reclaiming the Center: Confronting Evangelical Accommodation in Postmodern Times*, ed. Paul K. Helseth, Millard J. Erickson, and Justin Taylor. Wheaton, Ill.: Crossway, 2004. I examine and critique the view that we are inside language and cannot get "outside," and then I apply my findings to the postmodern attacks on foundationalism. I consider not only the views of Hauerwas, Kallenberg, Grenz, and Franke, but also of Nancey Murphy. (I, A)

————. "Post-Conservatives, Foundationalism, and Theological Truth: A Critical Evaluation." In *Journal of the Evangelical Theological Society*,

48:2 (2005). I explore and critique the common postmodern critiques of foundationalism, as understood by Nancey Murphy. I also briefly defend how we can know objective truth. (I)

———. "Postmodernism and the Priority of the Language-World Relation." In *Christianity and the Postmodern Turn,* ed. Myron Penner. Grand Rapids, Mich.: Brazos, 2005. In my second essay in this book, I reply to the first essays by my fellow contributors, and I go on to begin to develop my own case that we do indeed have access to the objective world. I also explore briefly the implications of their philosophical views for certain essential Christian doctrines. (I)

———. Review of *Beyond Foundationalism: Shaping Theology in a Postmodern Context,* by Stanley Grenz and John Franke (Louisville: Westminster/John Knox, 2000). *Philosophia Christi* 5:2 (2004). (I)

———. Review of *Natural and Divine Law: Reclaiming the Tradition for Christian Ethics,* by Jean Porter (Grand Rapids, Mich.: Eerdmans, 1999). *Philosophia Christi* 3:2, 2001. Porter advocates a return to Thomistic ethics, but in so doing she recasts it in a postmodern, linguistic approach. (I)

———. "Some Conceptual Problems for Hauerwas's Virtue Ethics." In *Philosophia Christi* 3:1, 2001. (I)

———. *Virtue Ethics and Moral Knowledge: Philosophy of Language After MacIntyre and Hauerwas.* Aldershot, England: Ashgate, 2003. This is my in-depth, philosophical critique of the central ideas behind MacIntyre, Kallenberg, and Hauerwas's views (and, by extension, many of Murphy's, Grenz's, Franke's, and Jones's). I also develop a chapter on implications of their proposals for Christian theology, as well as the implications for the frequently made charge of relativism. (A)

Willard, Dallas. "A Crucial Error in Epistemology." *Mind* 304 (October 1967): 513-523. (A)

———. "How Concepts Relate the Mind to Its Objects: The 'God's Eye View' Vindicated." *Philosophia Christi,* Series 2, 1:2 (1999): 5-20. This essay is a main statement of how we know the real world. It could be one of the most significant essays in philosophy in at least the last ten years. (A)

RELATIVISM

Beckwith, Francis J., and Greg Koukl. *Relativism: Feet Firmly Planted in Mid-Air.* Grand Rapids, Mich.: Baker, 1998. This excellent book is not only accessible but it also provides a strong set of reasons why relativism is mistaken. Koukl is the founder of the apologetics ministry Stand to Reason, and Beckwith is a leading Christian philosopher and apologist. (B, I)

Copan, Paul. *True for You, But Not for Me.* Minneapolis: Bethany, 1998. This is an excellent set of short essays that address a variety of slogans people offer, which all too often leave Christians speechless. (B, I)

Harris, James. *Against Relativism*. Peru, Ill.: Open Court, 1992. This is a sophisticated philosophical argument against relativism in its many forms. (A)

Koukl, Greg. "Responding to Relativism." Lecture given at Biola University for the Defending the Faith Lecture Series. This taped lecture is available through Biola University's Apologetics program. Koukl gives many lucid examples of how to address people who espouse the relativist's line of thought. (B, I)

Pojman, Louis P. "Ethical Relativism: Who's to Judge What's Right or Wrong?" Chapter in *Ethics: Discovering Right and Wrong*. 2nd ed. Belmont, Mass.: Wadsworth, 1990. This is a fine piece by a secular, well-respected philosopher who shows that ethical relativism is baseless, and that there must exist at least some objective moral norms. (I)

Religious relativism (pluralism):

Netland, Harold. *Religious Pluralism*. Downers Grove, Ill.: InterVarsity Press, 2001. (I, A)

OBJECTIVITY OF KNOWLEDGE

Willard, Dallas. *Logic and the Objectivity of Knowledge*. Athens: Ohio University Press, 1984. This probably is the most complete, contemporary defense of our knowledge of objective truth. (A)

GENERAL APOLOGETICS: THE CASE FOR THE EXISTENCE OF GOD AND THE TRUTH OF CHRISTIANITY

Craig, William Lane. *Reasonable Faith*. Rev. ed. Wheaton, Ill.: Crossway, 1994. This is an excellent survey text we use at Biola in our Defending the Faith lecture series. (I, A)

Craig, William Lane, and J. P. Moreland. *Philosophical Foundations of a Christian Worldview*. Downers Grove, Ill.: InterVarsity Press, 2003. This is a textbook on Christian philosophy written by two of the best Christian philosophers and apologists of our time. It includes sections on metaphysics, epistemology, ethics, philosophy of science, and philosophy of religion. Chapter 6 addresses postmodernism. (I)

Geivett, Doug. *Evil and the Evidence for God*. Philadelphia: Temple University Press, 1993. Geivett gives an excellent defense of the Christian faith in light of the challenges posed by the problem of evil. Significantly, he argues that the problem of evil should be situated in light of arguments that already have established God's existence. He offers two excellent chapters that out-line a cumulative case argument for God's existence.

Habermas, Gary R., and Michael Licona. *The Case for the Resurrection of Jesus.* Grand Rapids, Mich.: Kregel, 2004. (B, I)

Moreland, J. P. *Scaling the Secular City.* Grand Rapids, Mich.: Baker, 1987. Though it was written several years ago, Moreland's arguments for God's existence, religious experience, and more are very pertinent and powerful. I find his moral argument for God's existence extremely helpful in its cogency and scope of issues considered. (I, A)

Wright, N. T. *The Resurrection of the Son of God.* Minneapolis: Augsburg/Fortress, 2003. (A)

INDEX